EVERYMAN'S HISTORY OF THE ENGLISH CHURCH

BRITONS SHELTERING A CHRISTIAN MISSIONARY.—By W. Holman Hunt.

EVERYMAN'S HISTORY

OF THE

ENGLISH CHURCH

By

Percy Dearmer, D.D.

With 114 Illustrations

A. R. MOWBRAY & CO. LTD.
LONDON : 28 Margaret Street, Oxford Circus, W. 1
OXFORD : 9 High Street.

First impression, 1909
New edition, 1919
New impression, 1921

CONTENTS

LIST OF ILLUSTRATIONS

ix

LIST OF ILLUSTRATIONS XV

B

Everyman's History of the English Church

❧✝❧

CHAPTER 1

THE DAWN OF THE FAITH

THE Christian Faith first established itself in Britain among the Gaulish merchants and Roman soldiers who came over to our island. Its existence here is mentioned by Tertullian, so that c. 208 probably Christian congregations had become established here and there before the end of the 2nd century. During the 3rd and 4th centuries this ancient British Church must have been small and insignificant; few traces of it exist in history, and hardly a single Christian emblem of this period has been discovered by our archæologists. But a few years ago Sir W. St. John Hope unearthed the foundations of a tiny Christian church while excavating the site of the ancient Roman city of Silchester, near Reading. This church is probably

PLAN OF SILCHESTER CHURCH.

3

as early as the 3rd century : its altar is at the west end, following the ceremonial of the primitive Church, in which the celebrant stood behind the altar and thus faced east.

St. Alban

304 ? The story of St. Alban, the proto-martyr of Britain, comes to us from a strong and very early tradition, and there is thus no reason for disbelieving it.[1] But, as the persecution of the Emperor Diocletian in 304 did not reach Britain, it is likely that Bede was wrong when he tells us that St. Alban was martyred then : this was the last of the persecutions, and we may therefore surmise that St. Alban died in the 3rd century under one of the previous persecutions.

The story is that Alban, while still a pagan, gave refuge for charity's sake to a Christian priest who was flying from his persecutors. He concealed the priest in his house for some days, and during that time was so impressed by his guest's beautiful character that

THE MARTYRDOM OF ST. ALBAN.

[1] When St. German (see p. 10) visited Verulam in 429, he found the people worshipping at the shrine of St. Alban, and took back some dust from the tomb for a church which he built at Auxerre in honour of the martyr.

he set himself to learn his secret, was converted, and baptized. At last the soldiers came. Alban went to the door disguised in the *amphibalus*, the chasuble-shaped cloak [1] of the priest, and gave himself up in his stead. The judge recognized Alban, who then declared himself publicly to be a Christian. He was led up the flowery hill of Verulam on to "a most beautiful plain," where, Bede says, the soldier appointed for his execution was himself converted, and was beheaded after Alban, "baptized by the washing of his own blood." Verulam came to be called after its famous martyr ; and we know it still as St. Albans in Hertfordshire.

The Roman Empire becomes Christian

It was at York, on British soil, that Constantine the Great was proclaimed Emperor by the troops, in 306. His father, the Caesar Constantius Chlorus (that is, "Constantius the Pale") had been governor of Britain ; though there is no foundation for the story that his mother, St. Helena, was a British lady. Gradually Constantine overcame his rivals, and became sole Emperor of Rome. At the critical moment of his fortunes, he had the famous vision of the Cross, with the words, "By this conquer," which was seen not only by him but also by the whole army. This led him to take the side of the religion which only eight years before had been so cruelly persecuted. Next year he issued that great Edict of Toleration which brought the Church within the pale of the law ; and soon afterwards Christianity instead of Paganism became the official religion of the Roman Empire. Thus in the

312

313

[1] Like that worn by St. Augustine in picture on page 19.

civilized Britain of the 4th century Christianity became the dominant faith.

314   We know that three British bishops attended the Council of Arles just after Constantine's edict—a Bishop of London, named Restitutus, a Bishop of York, and another who was probably Bishop of Lincoln. The names of all three, with those of their attendant priest and deacon, are preserved. No doubt the British Church gradually in this century spread the Faith from the Roman soldiers and officials to the native Britons ; but we know nothing of these early missionaries. We only know that the Church was so poor that the British

359   bishops who attended the Council of Rimini were glad to have their expenses paid by the Emperor.

401   At the beginning of the next century a momentous event occurred. The Roman legions were withdrawn, and Britain was left to herself.

CHAPTER 2

PIONEERS TO OTHER PEOPLES

THE BRITISH MISSIONARY AGE

BUT, while the mighty Empire of Rome was slowly crumbling away before the invasions of the Barbarians, the British Church had begun a great missionary work. Thrown upon their own resources, the Celts developed splendid centres of light and learning, whence bands of devoted monks spread the Faith.

St. Ninian

Before the end of the 4th century **397** St. Ninian, "the Apostle of the Picts," went forth to preach the Gospel among the natives of what is now the south-west of Scotland: he built a stone church in honour of St. Martin of Tours (whose disciple he had probably been), and the rude Picts, accustomed only to wooden huts, called it the "white house," whence the place is still Whithern in Wigtown-shire to this day.[1]

ST. NINIAN.

Next among these British missionaries must be mentioned St. David, and St. Patrick the most renowned of all.

[1] "Hern" or "horn" = Anglo-Saxon *ærn*, a house.

7

St. David

c. 450   Of St. David little historical is known ; but his work among the people of Wales made a deep and enduring impression, as the very name " Taffy " (i.e. David) bears witness to-day, and he has always been the patron saint of the country. He was born at Menevia, now called St. Davids after him, and he had many saintly followers, whose strange names are still commemorated in Welsh parish churches, as well as in Brittany, where they also laboured.

St. Patrick

St. Patrick was not an Irishman, but probably a
(c. 390) native of Britain who studied in Gaul. It is said that he was born near the Severn mouth ; and his family takes us back to the beginnings of Christianity in Britain, since both his father and grandfather had been of the clergy. At the age of sixteen he was taken captive in some piratical raid, and was brought a slave to Antrim. There he got to know the Irish people, who were then in the darkness of heathendom. He escaped, and after-wards came back as a missionary among the people he
c. 463 had learnt to love. There after a wonderful and heroic life he died, having, with the aid of St. Bridget and other disciples, founded the Scottish Church in Ireland.

And here we must explain why this *Irish* Church, to which we Anglo-Saxons owe so much, has to be called the *Church of the Scots* or the Scottish Church. The Scots were originally an Irish race ; but they afterwards gave their name to North Britain, because a colony of Christian Scots emigrated from Ireland later on in the 5th century and founded a kingdom in what we now call Scotland. At the time of which we are writing Ireland was called

Scotia, and the Scottish Church was the Church of Ireland with a vigorous offshoot growing up on the British side of the Channel.

A Heresy and a Revival

St. German and St. Lupus

Meanwhile Britain distinguished itself in the 5th century by giving birth to a heresy. In 358 St. Hilary had congratulated the British Church on its orthodoxy, in 363 St. Athanasius had specially mentioned the Britons as being loyal to the Nicene Creed ; St. Chrysostom and St. Jerome had also borne witness to the Catholicism of Britain. But early in the 5th century the Church was distracted by the heresy of *Pelagius*, who was himself a British priest, his real name being the still familiar Welsh or British one of Morgan, which he translated into the classical form of Pelagius. He lived abroad, but a disciple of his brought into Britain the heresy (of which still to-day

St. German and St. Lupus.

many " Pelagians do vainly talk "), which practically denies original sin and asserts that a man can lead a holy life by the mere power of his own will.

The simple Britons were not able to cope with the Pelagians in argument : so they applied to Gaul for help ; and the Gallican bishops sent them two famous missionaries, St. German or Germanus, Bishop of Auxerre, and **429-447** St. Lupus, Bishop of Troyes. These two good men not only confuted the Pelagians but effected a great religious revival in Britain.

It so happened that while they were here the Picts and Saxons invaded the land. The British warriors met them in Wales. Our native Christianity must **430** have been in need of the teaching from Gaul, for most of the army had not been baptized. This was done on Easter Even ; and the soldiers went out at Eastertide, still wearing the white robes of their baptism, to meet the foe. German told them to repeat what he and Lupus should say. Then, when the enemy advanced, they cried "Alleluya" with a mighty shout that reverberated among the rocks of the Welsh valley ; and the heathens fled in terror. This was the bloodless " Alleluya Victory."

CHAPTER 3

THE HEATHEN ENGLISH

The Coming of the English

NOW the British Church was not long to enjoy peace. 449 Hardly had German and Lupus gone back to Gaul, when certain daring pirates, who had long been marauding in the British Channel, gained a footing in the Isle of Thanet. They were Jutes from the North German land still called Jutland— the first of our English race to lay hold on Britain. After them came the other two tribes from Germany, the Angles and the Saxons : fishermen, hunters, and farmers they were, driven by the need of expansion to become freebooters and colonists by force in poor, unprotected Britain. They were heathen, and we still use the names of their gods every time we mention any day of the week. Collectively they even then called themselves by the name of the dominant tribe of the Angles : so Britain became *England,* while some districts bore the Saxon name east, south, middle, and west, in Essex, Sussex, Middlesex, and 449 c. 590 Wessex. All this took nearly a century and a half,

An Anglo-Saxon
Thegn.

while the hapless Britons were slain, or enslaved, or driven westward to the inaccessible fastnesses of the Welsh mountains, or to the remote safety of the wild lands between Glastonbury and the Land's End, or even across the Channel to France, where they gave their name to Brittany.

To this time belongs the beautiful but shadowy figure of King Arthur, with his knights of the
500   Round Table. Some great and chivalrous Christian warrior of that name there probably was; but the glorious romance which was woven round his name in the Middle Ages is a poem and nothing else, bearing dim witness to some forgotten tradition of these troubled times.

And England, as we may now call it, was a heathen land once more. The British Church never recovered from that terrible extermination. It continued to exist in the west, where it did a great work. Even in heathen England a few Christian congregations struggled on;
580   and there seems to have been a British Bishop of London almost up to the coming of St. Augustine—tiny smouldering embers in the prevailing darkness of heathenism.

The Scottish Church of Ireland

But in the comparative safety of Ireland the younger Church of the Scots flourished exceedingly. There the lamp of civilization burnt with peculiar brightness; great homes of education were established, where learning, art, and religion flourished. The monks of Ireland won for it the name of the Island of Saints.

Christendom at this time consisted not only of the *Eastern* Churches which centred at Constantinople and the ancient patriarchates in Syria and Egypt, and of the

Western Churches which centred at Rome, but also of the *North-western* Churches of Ireland and of Britain, which were Celtic and centred nowhere in particular.

Small, splendid, and romantic, the Scottish Church spread its influence unrestingly, with little organization, with its own customs and liturgies, its own time of keeping Easter, and even (as in the picture on p. 15) its own clerical tonsure that distinguished at a glance its monks and clergy from those of the West, who shaved their heads in a ring (Illus. p. 19), and from those of the East, who shaved off their hair altogether. It was a Church that salted the earth.

The End of the British Church

And salt was needed sorely; for heathen England had to be converted. The persecuted and shrunken British Church could not do this, strong though it was in Wales, where it had fine centres of learning and a loyal people. Indeed the British Church did nothing to convert its conquerors, whom it despised as barbarians and hated with a bitterness that we can understand. And it was not only separated from its heathen neighbours, but also from the growing power of Christian Rome because of the different customs which it shared with the Scottish Church. When Augustine came to England a little later, he sought to impose his authority on the British bishops at two meetings near Wales. They refused to submit to the Archbishop of the hated English, and went on, separate, with their own customs: three more centuries were to elapse before the last adherents of the **c. 900** British Church became one with the Church of England.

So we close the history of the British Church, and return to the Church of the Scots.

CHAPTER 4

THE CONVERSION OF THE ENGLISH

HOW were the Anglo-Saxons to be converted? God ordained that this should be done by two very different agencies, each coming from opposite directions, the Scottish Mission from the north-west, and the Roman Mission from the south-east.

THE MISSION FROM THE NORTH

St. Columba

563 First came the Scottish Mission to Britain. Columba left Ireland, in company with a body of monks, and established a monastery in the little Isle of Iona, on the west coast of what is now called Scotland. His mission was to his fellow Scots, whose religion had weakened, and also to the heathen Picts among whom they dwelt ; but his monastery of Iona was destined to become a great missionary college of signal influence, whence the light was to shine in ever-spreading rays across the North of Britain.

Columba was not the first of those Northern missionaries. St. Ninian's mission, now a century and a half old, was still remembered, and its *White Church* (Withern) stood then, and for long afterwards, as a witness of the dawn of the Faith among the Picts. But the power of St. Columba's simplicity and fervour were to make of Iona the "Mother Church" of Englishmen as well as of Picts.   There Columba worked with a hundred and fifty monks, each living in his little bee-hive shaped hut. These huts all centred round the church, and were protected by an enclosure : the monks farmed, and fished, and copied books, and studied, but, above all, they spent much time in prayer. It is said that Columba would go out at night and stand immersed in the sea, reciting all the psalms one after the other ; for all monks knew the Psalter by heart. These monks had nothing of their own, but all things were common :

St. Columba at Iona.

they were hospitable to all who came, and they loved both man and beast.   Thus they preached the Gospel by living the Gospel.   To these Celtic monks came two Saxons, the first-fruits of our English race for Christ.

St. Columba worked for thirty-four years at Iona. In the year that he died St. Augustine arrived in Kent.

597

The Mission from the South

It was the Roman Mission that achieved the first great conversion, before the Mission of the Scots had penetrated amongst the English people. In the memorable year 597 the prior of a certain monastery in Rome, Augustine by name, arrived in the Isle of Thanet. The way had been prepared by Divine providence. Ethelbert, the King of Kent, was no ordinary monarch : strong and broad-minded, he was the first of our tribal English rulers to exercise supremacy over the other Anglo-Saxon kingdoms. The English, as a whole, were beginning to settle down, and were outgrowing the paganism of their earlier days. Moreover, Ethelbert had married a Frankish princess, famous now as Queen Bertha, who was a Christian, and who had brought over a bishop, Luithard ; so that already there was a little body of communicants at Canterbury, before Augustine came.

St. Gregory the Great

Meanwhile one of the greatest men who ever sat on a bishop's throne had been watching for his opportunity. St. Gregory the Great, one of the real founders of what we may henceforth call the Papacy, had seen the slave children from Northumbria twelve years before, when he, a wealthy young praetor of noble birth, had already given away all his goods to the poor, and had changed his silk and jewels for the rough cloak of a monk. The story is known to every schoolboy. Let us give it here in words taken from a version which has been published during the present year :

> " It fell one morn in Rome twelve years ago,
> An Abbot, Gregory the Deacon, fared,
> Watching the traffic of the market-place.
> And, as he stood and mused upon the scene, .
> He saw a little band of children slaves—
> Fair-haired—like these—among that swarthy crowd,

Poor tender lambs, torn from their distant homes
For alien bondage ! To the dealer, then—
'Tell me,' he said, 'whence come these innocents ?'
'Men call them Angles,' answer gave the man.
'Angles !' the deacon said, and touched their cheeks,
Ruddy, and compassèd with golden hair,
'Angles ! nay, *Angels*, rather be they called,
Since God's own hosts no lovelier are than these.
And what the land where men like Angels grow ?'
'Deira, in tar Northumberland.' But he—
'Deira, well-omened name ! for from God's wrath
We'll save the race that blossoms in such guise.
Have they a King ?' 'Yea, Ælla is his name.'
'Ælla ! Well named, for now his race shall sing
To Jesus Alleluya !'"

St. Augustine of Canterbury

Gregory did not forget that day. Indeed he started to go himself as missionary to the English ; but those were troublous times in Rome, and because the people could not spare him, they sent after him and fetched him back. Ten years later they made him their bishop. Then Pope Gregory chose Augustine for the mission.

Augustine landed in Kent with about 40 monks and some Frankish interpreters. After a few days, King Ethelbert came out to meet the missionaries. They carried in procession a silver cross together with a wooden banner on which the Crucifixion was painted ; and Augustine told the King and his thegns " how the tender-hearted Jesus by His own throes had redeemed the sinful world, and opened the kingdom of heaven to all believers." The King listened courteously, but acted with characteristic English caution : he told the missionaries that he could not yet agree to their strange and new words, or accept their promises, beautiful but unproved ; still they were

c

free to live in Canterbury, and make converts if they could.

So to Canterbury they went, entering the city in procession to the strains of the *Deprecamur*—"We beseech thee, O Lord, turn thine anger and wrath from this city and from thy holy house, for we have sinned. Alleluya ! " They used Bertha's church of St. Martin for their worship, and by their beautiful and Christian lives they soon won converts. In a few months Ethelbert himself was baptized. The Church was founded among the English : Augustine went to Gaul to be made a bishop, and thus became the first Archbishop of Canterbury.

Slow progress

We must not imagine, however, that England had been converted, because we nowadays think of the Archbishop of Canterbury as head of the English Church.

604 or 605 Augustine, when he died, had established Christianity in Kent, had founded a bishopric at Rochester and a mission outpost among the East Saxons of London ; but the Bishop of London, Mellitus, was afterwards driven out. Thus Augustine was practically Archbishop of Kent only ; and

616 here also there was a relapse ; for King Ethelbert's own son and successor ruled at first as a heathen. The original plan of organizing the English Church on the plan of the ancient British Church, with archbishoprics at London and York, never came about ; and, because of London's heathenism just then, it is still to-day not a metropolitan city in the proper sense of the word.

And what of York and northern England ? A bishopric was soon founded there, as we shall see ; but it did not bring about the conversion of the North. Bit

St. Augustine before King Ethelbert.—By G. E. Kruger-Gray.

by bit the Gospel spread among the English settlements; but there were many heathen reactions, and we must not think that missionary work won a sudden and universal success, any more than it had done in the days of the Apostles or of the early Fathers—any more than it does at the present day. People sometimes imagine that once upon a time missionaries had a magical success and that nowadays they are doing very little. This is not at all true. Those early gospellers to England gave up houses and lands and everything to serve Christ, and lived lives of incredible hardness ; yet many more heathen have been converted by Englishmen alone during the last hundred years than were converted by the Roman and Scottish missionaries during the hundred years after the coming of Augustine. It took nearly a century to make that small and scattered English population Christian, for the evangelization of the South Saxons did not begin till St. Wilfrid preached amongst them in 681.

The first preaching to the Northern English came about in this wise.

The Story of King Edwin

616   There was a young Northumbrian prince living in exile, called Edwin.[1] He was the son of that Aella, King of Deira, of whom Gregory had heard in Rome. While he was staying with Raedwald, King of East Anglia, messengers came from the Northumbrian King who had driven Edwin out, offering Raedwald this choice —a large bribe if he would slay his young guest, or war

---

[1] The name was then spelt Eadwine, and pronounced German fashion in four syllables. Ethelbert's name was spelt Aethelberht, and pronounced Athelbert ; so too Aella was pronounced Alla. Alfred was spelt Aelfred, and therefore pronounced as now.

if he refused. Raedwald, by the way, had become a queer kind of half-Christian : he had a temple with a Christian and a heathen altar side by side—which was undenominationalism with a vengeance. Now he gave way, and agreed to do the murder. But one of his thegns went to Edwin's bedroom, led him out into the darkness, and there told him of the plot. Edwin refused to escape : " I will still trust Raedwald," he said, "for he has been kind to me ; but if I must die, let my death come from him, and from no meaner man. And whither could I flee, after so many years of exile ?" Then he sat down, sorrowful and alone.

As Edwin wondered what he should do, a tall figure, strangely clad, came near him in the darkness ; and he began to be afraid. "Why art thou sitting here," asked the stranger, "while others sleep ?" "What is that to thee ?" said Edwin ; but the stranger told him that he knew his trouble, and asked him what he would give to the man who saved him ; and what more if he were to become a great king, greater than all the other kings of the English. "All that I had," said Edwin. "And what," pursued the stranger, "if he asked thee to take his counsel, and

PAULINUS AND KING EDWIN.

live a better and a happier life than thy forefathers ever dreamt of. Wouldst thou obey him?" "I would follow his teaching in all things," said Edwin. Then the stranger laid his hand on Edwin's head, and said, "When this sign shall be given thee, remember, and fulfil thy promise." Edwin did not know that the stranger was Paulinus, one of Augustine's monks.

Some influence was brought to bear on Raedwald, who now suddenly turned against the Northumbrian King and accepted his offer of war. He and Edwin **616** defeated their enemy in a fierce battle; and soon Edwin became King of Northumbria, and a greater overlord of all Britain than any king had been before, or was to be again for many a generation. He gave his name to Edinburgh or Edwinsburgh, so that the capital of Scotland still records his prowess to-day; but York was his capital, and there he ruled with the state of a Roman emperor, with banners carried before him when he rode abroad with his nobles.

625 King Edwin married Ethelburga, the Christian daughter of Ethelbert; and, as her mother, Bertha, had done, she brought a bishop with her as chaplain. The bishop was Paulinus. But Edwin was still a Pagan. For nearly a year Queen Ethelburga and Paulinus prayed without result.

Then on Easter Even an envoy came with a message **626** from the King of Wessex, but treacherously, with a poisoned dagger. As Edwin gave him audience, he drew the dagger from under his garment to slay him; but a faithful thegn, named Lilla, threw himself as a shield before the King. The dagger struck Lilla to the death, and passing right through his body wounded his master. That night the Queen bare Edwin a daughter. Then Edwin gave thanks to his gods that she and he had

both come that day safely through the peril of death.
But Paulinus stood by, and said that his thanks were due
to our Lord ; and Edwin was moved, and promised that
the babe should be given to Christ, and that he too would
serve God if he conquered in his coming battle against
the King of Wessex.   On Whitsun Eve the little princess
was baptized together with eleven of her attendants, the
first-fruits of Northumbria for Christ.   Edwin returned
victorious ; but still he hesitated ; " being a man of extraordinary sagacity," says Bede, " he often sat alone by
himself a long time, silent as to his tongue, but delibe-
rating in his heart how he should proceed."

One day, as he sat thus alone, Paulinus came up to him.
" Dost thou remember the sign ?" he asked, and laid his
hand upon his head. Edwin started, and would have fallen
at his feet ; but Paulinus took his hand and bade him remember his promise.   Then Edwin said he was ready, and
would summon his Wise Men to consider the matter.

They met at Goodmanham in the East Riding, and   627
the King asked them one by one what they thought of
the new religion.   " None," said Coifi the priest, " have
served the gods more busily than I, but there is no virtue
in it ; they have brought me no profit.   Were these gods
good for anything they would help their worshippers."

Higher words spoke an aged noble :—

" O King, this present life of man, compared with that time
beyond which is unknown to us seems to me like this : When you are
sitting with your aldermen and thanes at supper in winter time, with a
bright fire burning in the midst of the hall, while outside the rain and
snow are beating against the walls—lo ! a sparrow flies swiftly in at one
door, and swiftly through the hall, and out at another.   He was safe for
a moment from the wintry storm while he was indoors, but after that
short spell of warmth he disappears.   From winter he came in, and to
winter he goes out.   Such is the life of man : he appears for a little

while. But what went before? And what will follow after? This we do not know. Therefore, if this new teaching bring us anything more sure, it is worth our following."

The others spoke to like effect. Then Paulinus, swarthy and gaunt Paulinus, stood up in the midst of the fair-haired Angles and preached. When he had made an end, "The more I sought for truth in our religion," said Coifi the priest, "the less I found it. But here is the truth that will give us life and salvation. Wherefore I advise, O King, that we set fire to our temples." "Who will be the first?" cried Edwin. "I," said Coifi the priest,

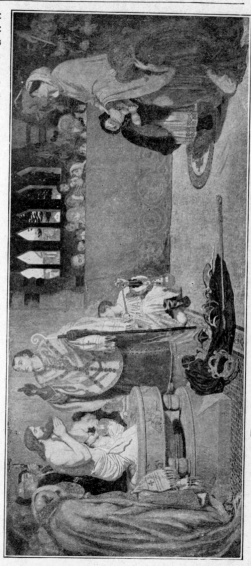

THE BAPTISM OF KING EDWIN.—By Ford Madox Brown.

" I, who worshipped most the idols, should be the first to destroy." Then they rode to the temple, and Coifi cast his spear at it, while all the people wondered and thought him mad. They burnt it and all that was in it with fire; and then Edwin returned to York. A rough church was hastily built of wood : there on Easter Even, 627, the King at last was christened. On that spot now stand the glorious walls of York Minster.

The Deacon James and Paulinus

There was with Paulinus a deacon called James, one of those indomitable heroes who are of all men most serviceable to humanity. The two travelled up and down over the wild country from the Firth of Forth to the Cheviots, and even southward beyond the Humber as far as Lincoln, baptizing converts wherever they went.

But the reign of their great and good King was soon ended. A terrible warrior, *Penda*, King of Mercia (the middle of England), came forward as the champion of heathenism, allied himself with Cadwallon, an unworthy Christian British King, slew Edwin at the battle of Heathfield, and ravaged Northumbria, torturing and slaying the people. Paulinus fled to the sea, and sailed with the widowed Ethelburga and her children to Kent, where he became Bishop of Rochester, and subsequently the Queen became a nun. But the deacon James did not leave. He went about, through all the slaughter and apostasy, making Christians. Thirty years later we find him, " extraordinarily skilful in singing," still at his post. He is one of the many saints who have never been canonized.

633

The Scottish Mission Again

And now a new power appears in North England, and St. Columba's Mission at Iona comes into play among the English, just when the pioneer work of the Italian Paulinus seemed to have failed. The Roman Mission had broken up more ground in various parts of England since Augustine had died in 604 ; but such a small handful of men could not accomplish more, and they were dwindling in numbers.[1] But an inexhaustible supply of missionaries was to flow in from Iona, first into Northumbria, and then into the other unconverted parts of England. The first opportunity of the Scottish monks came in a remarkable manner, just when Northumbria lay waste under the swords of Penda and Cadwallon.

St. Oswald

It is another story of an exile, in this age of warring English kingdoms, and again King Raedwald was the unconscious pivot of great events. He had in 617 killed the father of Oswald (the king who had sought Edwin's life), and Oswald, then only twelve years old, took refuge with some companions in Iona, and there was baptized and taught the Faith.

ST. OSWALD.

[1] The last of them was Honorius, who lived on till 653, having been Archbishop of Canterbury since 628.

And now, about a year after King Edwin's death, Oswald came forward and raised the standard of Christ among the stricken Northumbrians. They rallied to him; and when he had a small army he went bravely out to meet the great host of Cadwallon at the Battle of Heavenfield, near Hexham. The night before the battle, **634 or** as Oswald lay down fully armed to rest, he had a vision **635** of his own saint, Columba, a shining figure that reached

HEAVENFIELD : BEFORE THE BATTLE.

to the sky and stood in the midst of the camp.[1] "Give battle at once," said Columba, "and the Lord will deliver the foe into your hand." Then Oswald roused his sleeping army, and in the night they made a cross of wood and dug a hole upon a little hill. Oswald himself held up the cross while the earth was shovelled in about it; and when it was fixed, he called upon all his soldiers to kneel—"Let us pray to the true God that He will deliver us from our cruel enemy. For He knows that our cause is just." Then at the

[1] Oswald himself told this to Failbhe, the eighth Abbot of Iona; and the ninth abbot, Adamnan, took it from him and wrote it in his life of Columba.

break of dawn they fell upon the foe, and won a great victory. The place where the cross stood is still called St. Oswald's.

So Oswald became King of Northumbria. He was a true saint, humble, brave, lavish in giving, intensely devout, and so constant in prayer that he often spent half the night in chapel, and habitually sat with his hands spread open on his knees, as was his custom when communing with God.

St. Aidan

King Oswald at once set himself to make his people Christian. He naturally applied to the monks of Iona for a bishop. They sent Corman; but he could make nothing of the wild Northumbrians, and came back to Iona, declaring that they were impossible to move. The monks met sadly to discuss what they should do. At last a voice was heard: "Perhaps, brother, you were too severe with those unlearned men, and did not give them first the milk of more easy doctrine, leaving till later the strong meat of God's sublimer truths?" They all turned, and saw that it was a monk called Aidan who had spoken. "This is the man for the task!" they said; and they sent him to be King Oswald's bishop.

635 Oswald lived mostly at the royal house, Bamborough; and Aidan set up his bishop's seat in a monastery which he founded hard by at Lindisfarne, a barren island that is approached over the wet sand at low tide: it has come to be known as Holy Island, a name which few places have deserved so well. This was the first church that

was ever built in that part of the kingdom which we now call Northumberland.

Aidan was a man of extraordinary beauty of character, and for fifteen years he evangelized the country, tramping everywhere on foot, winning all hearts. At first he needed an interpreter, and the King himself used to go with him and translate his sermons from the Irish tongue into English.

After eight happy years, the heathen Penda arose again, and slew Oswald at the Battle of Maserfield. 642 Aidan worked on for nine years longer, and then died. 651 At last, after having been responsible for the death of five Christian kings, Penda himself was slain at the Battle of Winwaed; and thus fell, in this decisive 655 battle, the last champion of paganism in England.

At his Holy Island Aidan had established a school for young laymen as well as a monastery. So indeed it was everywhere : Augustine had begun with a school at Canterbury ; and wherever the Church went, there went education also. The influence of Lindisfarne was immense ; monks who had been trained there went evangelizing southwards, and especially converted the Mercians in the middle of England, where Cedd worked under Penda's son, who had become a Christian. Cedd then went to the East Saxons and made London really Christian at last. Within thirteen years of Aidan's death all the kingdoms of England had received the Gospel, except Sussex, which was cut off by a dense forest.

But we cannot tell of all the saints who laboured in this heroic age. Even the famous St. Chad, the brother of Cedd, we can only mention, and the still more famous St. Cuthbert, the shepherd boy who had a

vision of Aidan's liberated soul on the night of his
death, and went straightway to become a monk and

St. Cuthbert at Lindisfarne.—By William Bell Scott.

missionary at Melrose, and was afterwards Prior of
Lindisfarne.

CHAPTER 5

THE SETTLEMENT OF THE ENGLISH CHURCH

NOW that the Gospel had been successfully preached nearly all over England, the time of settlement had come. With extraordinary devotion and courage, the missionaries had pressed in wherever an opening had occurred ; but, of course, the ground had been covered in a haphazard manner, and with little organization, among the different kingdoms that then made up England. There was no national unity, for there was no nation — only kingdoms of Northumbria, Kent, Mercia, Wessex, and the rest. It was the Church that first brought unity to England. This we owe under God to an Eastern monk, Theodore, who was, like St. Paul, a native of Tarsus.

But first another source of confusion had to be removed. England had been converted by two Missions, one Roman, the other Scottish (or Irish), which had no connection with each other. Each had a different spirit, a different system, different customs : the Scottish Church was essentially monastic—the monasteries sent out their bishops to perform episcopal functions, but it was the abbots who ruled. And the Scottish Church had its own tonsure, as we have seen, and its own time of keeping Easter. These may seem comparatively small matters, but it must have been intolerably distracting for a king to be celebrating Easter while his queen was in the middle of Passiontide.

St. Wilfrid

It was Wilfrid, the enthusiastic young abbot of Ripon, who
664 got these difficulties settled at the Conference of Whitby.
He had been born in the terrible year after King Edwin's
634 death : the son of a Northumbrian
noble, he grew up a handsome, brilliant
lad, fond of sport and arms and fine
clothes ; but he set his mind on religion
and made a pilgrimage to Rome with
another young noble, Benedict Biscop,
who was also to become a saint. In
Rome the lamp of an ancient civilization still burnt brightly, and the
glories of what had been the Empire
of the world mingled with the splendour of a growing spiritual power in
the great churches that now filled the
city. There Wilfrid found the highest
culture and the richest art, in contrast
with the rude provincial life of his
own half-civilized England. There
too he found a new monastic ideal

ST. WILFRID AT
WHITBY.

in the rule of St. Benedict, the founder of mediaeval
monasticism.[1] Wilfrid came home, determined to bring
the English Church into line with the rest of Western
civilization. He succeeded. A conference met in
St. Hilda's monastery at *Whitby* to decide which set
of customs was to be followed : the abbess, Hilda,
was there, on the side of the Scots, whose leader was

[1] Benedict died in 542.

Colman, the Bishop of Lindisfarne ; and two kings were there, and Bishop Cedd, and also Wilfrid, of course, the chief opponent of Colman. And there too we meet once more the good old deacon James, still at his post.

The Conference at Whitby settled that England should follow the ways of Rome, whereat Colman resigned his bishopric, and went off to live in Ireland. Thus ended the Mission of the Scots. No one doubts now that the Synod decided rightly. The English Church became one homogeneous body, and a sharer in the learning and art and civilization of the Continent.

We must be careful not to foul historical truth with modern controversial ideas. Rome then stood for progress, and it was good for England to follow her ways. Rome also stood for unity. A modern Anglican has no more right to deny what we owed to her then, than a modern Romanist has a right to say that because she did so much for Europe once, therefore the English Church ought to have followed her in all the mistakes she made afterwards. She does not now stand for progress, as she did then ; nor for unity, since her subsequent attempts at absolutism were a main cause of the schisms between East and West in the 11th century, and between her and half Europe in the 16th. But in the 7th century she was the link between the old civilization and the new ; and she held the lamp aloft while the barbarians were wrecking the old order, as they surged and settled over Europe. We can share the enthusiasm of Wilfrid without thinking the Pope is infallible—and, after all, the Pope did not himself think he was infallible then. The present pretensions of Rome are merely the obsolete survivals of an age when her strength and supremacy were necessary to Europe. That they should

D

have survived so long is natural. That they will disappear, as Christendom recovers its unity in a fuller knowledge and a wider tolerance, is inevitable.

Archbishop Theodore

And now providentially the way was clear for a man who by a strange destiny came to us from the Eastern Church. Theodore of Tarsus was 67 when he arrived in England, and yet for close on 22 years he ruled with a freshness, strength, wisdom, and courage such as few men have ever shown. When he came, the English Church scarcely existed except in name. When he died, it was a fully-equipped and organized institution, arranged in dioceses much as it is to-day. The English Church, as

669

ANGLO - SAXON ARCHITECTURE.
BRIXWORTH CHURCH, C. 680.

(The triforium balusters were added later, when the church was gradually restored after the ravages of the Danes. These balusters are characteristic of late Anglo Saxon architecture, from c. 980.)

we know it now, is mainly the work of this great Archbishop of Canterbury; and under him the Church became the matrix of a united English nation.

He summoned a *Synod* at *Hertford*, the first occasion 673
on which the Church of England acted as a single body
—for Whitby had been only an informal Northumbrian
conference. At this Synod momentous laws were passed
giving order to the Church. Moreover, with all the
huge burden upon his shoulders, Theodore found time
to make what was practically a university at Canterbury,
and to teach in it himself, for he was a very learned
man.

One of his chief tasks was the subdivision of the huge
unwieldy dioceses which had been established in England ;
and here he came into collision with Wilfrid, who had
been made Bishop of the Northumbrians, with his see, 678
not at Celtic Lindisfarne, but at York. Theodore divided
this great diocese, as he divided others, and left Wilfrid
with only a quarter of his see. Wilfrid was very angry,
and appealed to Rome, being the first Englishman thus
to acknowledge a Papal supremacy. The Pope ordered
that Theodore should give him back the rest of his
diocese. Theodore stuck to his metropolitan authority,
and ignored the Papal decision. The King of Northumbria went further, and threw Wilfrid into prison.
Wilfrid never got back his territory ; after a noble and
adventurous life, during which he went as missionary to 678
Frisia,[1] and also completed the conversion of England
by at last evangelizing the men of Sussex, and after a 681
second banishment and restoration, he died Bishop of 709
Hexham.

[1] Now called Friesland in Holland.

CHAPTER 6

THE CHRISTIAN CIVILIZATION

THUS the heroic age of the English Church closes with great names, as it had begun. Augustine, Aidan, and Theodore stand for the founding, the spreading, and the establishment of the Church ; but many others as great and good bore splendid share in the work, and an unknown host of confessors and martyrs as well, whose names we shall not know till we go forth to join them.

It was almost, if not entirely, by monks that England was made Christian ; and we owe, in common with the rest of Europe, the deepest debt of gratitude to these good men, who converted the barbarian conquerors of Europe, preserved learning in their midst when rapine and war were surging all around, and also by their untiring manual labour turned the forests and waste places of Christendom into farms and orchards.

AN ANGLO-SAXON ABBESS.
(From a Renaissance picture.)

St. Hilda

One or two of the more famous names must be mentioned in this connection. St. Hilda reminds us that

there were nuns as well as monks ; and also of the remarkable fact that there were many double monasteries, a
house of monks and a house of nuns under one head,
and that it was the *abbess* who ruled over both. In
these days, when we hear of women's rights as something
very new, it is well to remember that Abbess Hilda ruled
and taught a great college of clergy at Whitby, which gave
England some of its best bishops. Hilda was a great-
niece of King Edwin, and she had been baptized with
him as a girl on that memorable Easter Even of 627.
When she died, Aelflaed, who had been vowed to God as † 680
a little princess after the decisive Battle of Winwaed,
succeeded her ; the good St. John of Beverley, Bishop of
York, was one of Abbess Aelflaed's monks.

Caedmon

But a more famous monk of Whitby was Caedmon,
the father of English poetry. He was only a neat-herd
who looked after the cattle at the monastery ; and when
men used to sing at their feasts, or " Ales," handing
round the harp from one to the other, he found himself
unable to improvise, and used to slink out in shame at
his incompetence. But one night his genius awoke in
this strange fashion :

"Now it so happed that at one tide he left the house where the
Ale was held, and went out to the neat-stall, the ward of which was that
night trusted to him. And when at fitting time he laid his limbs to
rest and slept, there stood by him in his dream some man, who hailed
and greeted him, and named him by his name, ' Caedmon, sing me
somewise ! ' Then answered he, and quoth, ' I cannot sing aught ;
and for that I could not, I went forth out of the Ale, and came hither.'
Then quoth he that was speaking to him, ' Yet must thou sing to me.'
Quoth he, ' What shall I sing ? ' Quoth he, ' Sing to me of the beginning of things.' When he got this answer, then 'gan he forthwith to

sing, in praise of God the Maker, verses and words which he had never heard. And the burden of them is this :

> ' Now shall we praise the Uprearer of the realm
> Of the high heaven, and the Maker's might,
> And His mind's wisdom, Father of the world ;
> Yea, of all wondrous workings He hath set
> The first forthcomings—Lord for evermore !
> He for earth's children roofed the round of heaven,
> And laid this lower earth, Holy in all,
> Guardian of men, great God for evermore.' " [1]

CAEDMON BEFORE ST. HILDA AT WHITBY ABBEY.
By C. O. Skilbeck.

[1] Translated from King Alfred's Anglo-Saxon version of Bede by C. J. Abbey, *Religious Thought in Old English Verse* (1892), p. 2. In the original Anglo-Saxon the first line is, NU WE SCEOLAN HERIAN HEOFON-RICHES WEARD.

Next day he was taken to Abbess Hilda, who, to prove his story, set him a passage of Scripture to turn into verse. Then he became a monk, and wrote a great store of famous poetry. The beautiful tale of his death is told in the fourth book of Bede's history.

St. Benedict Biscop

Caedmon gives us a glimpse of the life in one of those early convents. St. Benedict Biscop shows us another side of that life in his founding of the noble monasteries of Wearmouth and Jarrow. He made many journeys to Rome ; and we realize what a revelation continental culture must have been to our forefathers, when we read how he brought back books, relics, and ornaments, and also pictures, which he stretched on boards and fastened on the walls, to the delight of the simple English folk ; while, besides this, he got masons from Gaul to build in stone, and craftsmen to make glass for the windows. It is about this time that we hear of fine stone churches, with rows of columns, and rich plate, and hangings of scarlet and gold, and jewelled books of the Gospels written in gold on purple vellum.

674

The Venerable Bede

Another monk must be mentioned, one to whom we owe the best of our knowledge of early English history. Need I say that I mean that lovely and gentle saint the Venerable Bede ? He was amazingly learned, and the prince of historians because of his love of truth and his beautiful power of expression. He seized on the records of vital importance, proved them, and preserved them for ever. It is to Bede that we owe it that all histories of these times read like a collection of fine stories.

We find him first as a choir-boy of seven at Jarrow Monastery, when the plague had wrought such havoc among the monks that only the abbot and this

THE DEATH OF BEDE.—By William Bell Scott.

young chorister were left to sing the services. At Jarrow he lived all his life, writing, it is said, a hundred and fifty books, among them the *Ecclesiastical History*, to which we owe so much. At Jarrow he died, as he was giving to England its first edition of an English Bible. How well these early Christians knew how to die! The story is told by one of his monks, named Cuthbert:

"Next morning, the eve of Ascension Day, he ordered us to go on writing with all speed. And while the rest had gone to walk in the Rogation procession, one of us said, 'Dearest master, there is still one chapter wanting. Will it trouble thee to answer any more questions?' He answered, 'It is no trouble. Take thy pen and make ready, and write fast.'

"At three o'clock he said to me, 'I have some little articles of value in my desk, such as peppercorns, napkins, and incense. Run quickly and bring the priests of the monastery to me, that I may distribute among them the gifts which God has bestowed on me. The rich in this world give gold and silver and precious things; but I with joy give my brothers what God has given me.' He spoke to each of them, and asked them to pray and say Masses for him, which they promised; but they all mourned and wept, especially when he said they should see his face no more in this world. 'It is time,' he said, 'that I return to Him who formed me. I have lived long; the time of my dissolution draws nigh, and I desire to be dissolved and be with Christ.'

"He passed the day joyfully, till the shadows of the evening began to fall; and then the boy who was writing down his translation of St. John said, 'Dear master, there is yet one sentence to be written.'

"He answered, 'Write it quickly.' Soon after, the boy said, 'The sentence is finished now.'

"'Thou hast well said, it is finished! Raise my head in thy hands; for I wish to be facing the holy place where I was wont to pray, and as I lie to call upon my Father.'

"And so he lay on the pavement of his little cell, singing 'Glory be to the Father, and to the Son, and to the Holy Ghost.' And when he had named the Holy Ghost, he breathed his last, and so departed to the heavenly kingdom."

In the year of Bede's death York became an arch- **735** bishopric, and the English Church thus took the form it still has to-day.

The death of Bede is generally held to close our heroic period. But we must remember that other heroes lived after him. Such was St. Boniface, a monk of Crediton in Devonshire, the "Apostle of Germany," who carried the Gospel to our Teutonic brethren, became Arch-

743

bishop of Mainz, and

755

died a martyr in Friesland, where St. Wilfrid and St.

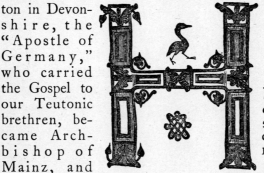

INCIPIT LIBER EXODVS

MS. of Alcuin. The beginning of Exodus.

Willibrord had laboured before him. Alcuin, the

† 804

greatest scholar of his day, also went to live in Germany, and was the friend and adviser of Charlemagne.

CHAPTER 7

DESTRUCTION AND RECOVERY

THE VIKINGS

IN the year 793 the Danish Vikings landed at Lindisfarne, and slew or enslaved the monks. Next year they fell upon Jarrow. They also raided Ireland; 793 794

THE LOOTING OF JARROW.—By C. O. Skilbeck.

they also destroyed Columba's holy place of Iona, slaying all the sixty-eight monks who were there. Forty years later these Scandinavian pirates began the invasion of Britain in earnest. Then the English suffered as once the Britons had suffered; for the Danes worshipped 827 71

How the Danes came up the Channel.—By Herbert A. Bone.
(By permission of Messrs. Cassell & Co. Ltd., London.)

Woden, as once the English had done, and slew Christian priests at the altar. Every river was a gateway for them into England : where they went, they slew, and pillaged, and burnt, till nearly all the learning and splendour that Christianity had given to England were swept away. York was stormed, and its religion submerged ; **867** St. Hilda's Abbey was destroyed—its very name of Whitby is Danish. We know hardly anything of what happened to the Archbishopric of York for the whole of the next hundred years. The See of Lindisfarne was destroyed, though its bishopric survived ; but the Bishoprics of Hexham and of Dunwich in Suffolk disappeared for ever ; others were broken for the best part of a century. In East Anglia the Danes pierced **870** with their arrows St. Edmund, King and Martyr, because he would not renounce Christ. It might have been well said of them—

> "The children born of thee are fire and sword,
> Red ruin, and the breaking-up of laws."

At first they came to plunder ; then they came to settle.

Alfred the Great

Fortunately King Egbert (802–31) had recently established a supremacy of Wessex, whose kings were destined to become the rulers of a united English nation. And now there arose a greater King of **871** Wessex, Alfred, who saved England from complete extermination and misery. His glorious struggles, and his **878** victory over the Danes at Ethandune, belong to other books than this. Here we note that after the Peace of Wedmore, the Viking chief, Guthrum, was baptized, and that King Alfred stood godfather to him. Then Guthrum

reigned north of Wessex as a Christian King, and
the Danish settlers rapidly became Christians. Thus
the invasion did in the end
extend the borders of the
Church.

But the Church was in
a sad plight. In North and
East England, which was
now the "Danelagh," the old
traditions and learning had
been irreparably destroyed.
Even in Alfred's own Wes-
sex, religion was at a low
ebb ; many of the priests
had been killed, and their
posts filled with inferior men ;
most of the monasteries had
been sacked and ruined, so
that monasticism was practically extinct. The books had
disappeared with the other
treasure. Ignorance was universal ; the poor were op-
pressed. Wessex itself had
lapsed into pitiful barbarism.

ALFRED·THE·KING

All this Alfred set him-
self to alter. Equally great
as a warrior, statesman, and
scholar, he was inspired by

ALFRED AND HIS FLEET.

the love of God. No failing marred the perfect balance
of his bright and sunny character ; no ruler has ever
showed as he did the identity of duty to God and to
his people. He is the pattern of a Christian king,

the perfect type, so seldom reached.   He was the regenerator of the Church, the hero and saviour of England, the real founder of our national greatness. No one is more worthy of the title " Saint " ; and when the English Church reforms her Kalendar the memory of Alfred will be given that long-deferred reward.

We cannot tell here all that he did.   Yet his wonderful industry never caused him to omit his daily

KING ALFRED'S
JEWEL.

(In the Ashmolean Mu-
seum, Oxford. On the
side it bears the name
AELFRED.)

worship at the Mass, or at the choir-services : he, who valued time so well that he invented measured candles to serve as clocks, always carried a Psalter and Prayer Book with him, and would go into his chapel secretly at night to pray.   We must remember him also as an educator who translated the best books, so that his people might have them in English ; and as a law-giver, who founded his code upon the law of God, bidding men live by the Golden Rule.   No wonder the Danes readily embraced Christianity when they saw what a man can be like who truly follows its precepts.   Alfred has been " England's Darling " [1] ever since, and is still an abiding inspiration after a thousand years.

After Alfred the recovery went on.   It was still † 900 sorely needed even in Wessex ; for we learn that at this time in the ancient monastery of Glastonbury Irishmen came over to give the teaching, because the English monks were all dead.   The Church revival of Alfred had raised the standard ; but there was amongst the clergy much

[1] This title was given him by an unknown writer of the 12th century.

comfortable, easy-going life, especially in the cathedral churches. A further revival was needed ; and it took the form of Benedictine monasticism.

St. Dunstan

959–
75

940

960

This became possible under the secure rule of another great king, Edgar the Peaceful, whose adviser was Dunstan, artist, statesman, saint, first a scholar at Glastonbury, then abbot in 940, then Archbishop of Canterbury and more than Prime Minister of England ; for Edgar, when he became King, at once turned out the former Arch- bishop and put Dunstan in his place. Dunstan is sometimes described as relentlessly attacking the married clergy ; but this is not true. He approved of the revival, but himself greatly moderated the zeal of the extreme reformers, among whom Edgar himself must be counted. He corrected the laxity of his own Canons at Canterbury, but did not put monks there. Forty Benedictine houses were established in the reign of Edgar, and the secular Canons were replaced by monks at the Cathedrals of Winchester and Worcester. Benedictinism proved a great regenerating force, then, and for long after. Indeed, though religious orders have always had periods of decay and recovery, it may be questioned whether the wise and humane reforms of St. Benedict (for such they were) will ever lose their vitality.

ST. DUNSTAN.

The Danes again

And now we must close the Anglo-Saxon period of our history, not pausing to tell the adventures of St. Dunstan, and his death, or how he caused pegs †988 to be set in the cups to stop excessive drinking, and ordered sermons to be preached every Sunday.

THE MARTYRDOM OF ST. ALPHEGE.—By C. O. Skilbeck.

Before he died, the Danes were upon us again. They 1012 killed St. Alphege, another Archbishop of Canterbury, in a drunken feast, because he would not take the money of the poor to pay for his ransom. But Cnut, 1017-35 the first Danish King of England, was a good Churchman and a wise man.

E

Close of the Anglo-Saxon Era

1043-65   The Saxon line was restored again in St. Edward the Confessor, the last King of Alfred's house, a pious man but a weak ruler, who founded Westminster Abbey, and also prepared the way for the next and last invasion of England.

But that invasion was to be the work of Churchmen. We have done with paganism.

KING CNUT AND QUEEN
EMMA FOUNDING A MONASTERY.

(From a contemporary MS.)

CHAPTER 8

THE NORMAN CONQUEST

WE have now just passed the middle point of our history. The Christian Faith has existed for a little over 1,700 years in this Island ; indeed the Pan-Anglican Congress of 1908 marked the seventeenth centenary of the first mention of British Christianity by Tertullian in 208. Of these seventeen centuries, about eight and a half come before the Battle of Hastings, and about eight and a half come after, thus :—

Tertullian	*Norman Conquest*	*Present Day*
A.D. 208...(858 years)...	A.D. 1066...(843 years)...	A.D. 1909.

William the Conqueror and Lanfranc

The Norman Conquest, after its opening horrors of **1066** bloodshed and devastation, proved to be a great boon for England. It had also a profound effect upon the English Church, which had grown slack and undisciplined, with a rather ignorant clergy, because isolated in a backwater from the stirring civilization of Europe. There now began again a period of 'grand ideals and noble ventures' which lasted till about the year 1300, a period of great men—of kings like William himself, Henry II, and Edward I, the makers of modern England, an age which produced Primates so eminent for sanctity, statesmanship, and learning, as Lanfranc (†1089),

Anselm (†1109), Theobald (†1161), Thomas à Becket (†1170), Hubert Walter (†1205), Stephen Langton (†1228), Edmund Rich (†1240).

Lanfranc, the most learned man of his age, the one friend and adviser who guided William's policy, had been originally a rich Italian lawyer at Pavia. When he was about thirty-five, he came to France, and set up at Avranches in Normandy a school to which men soon flocked from all parts of Europe. Suddenly, after pondering the words — "If any man will come after me, let him deny himself, and take up his cross, and follow me," he gave it all up. He went forth with one companion, not knowing whither he went. They were caught by robbers, stripped, and tied to a tree.

KNIGHT

Anno Domini
1170

G.E.K.

In the horror of the night, Lanfranc tried to say Lauds, found to his shame that he could not remember the service, and vowed that if he survived he would dedicate himself to God. He was released by some kindly men in the morning; and when he asked the way to the humblest monastery in those parts, they directed him to a little house which Herluin was building at Bec. Now Herluin was a simple-hearted soldier, who had retired from the army, and for years had been getting together a rough monastery, building it with his own hands: he had often prayed for some clever monk to come who would help in governing the rough, undisciplined men that formed his little community. Lanfranc was the answer to his prayers. Lanfranc, brilliant and famous, humbly submitted him-

self to the good old soldier, who had but lately taught himself to read; and he gave himself up to the hardships of the life. But, with Lanfranc there, Bec began to be known; and soon grew to be a great and famous abbey, filled with scholars.

William made great friends with Lanfranc, and set him as abbot of his new monastery, St. Etienne at Caen. A few years later when the Conqueror

EARLY NORMAN ARCHITECTURE.

1070

wanted a new Archbishop of Canterbury, in place of the Anglo-Saxon Stigand whom he had deposed, he sent to Lanfranc as the one man for the post, and forced him to come to England.

Soon all the bishoprics and most of the other places of power, in Church as well as in State, were occupied

by very competent foreigners. The Normans were keen
Churchmen, with a great sense of decency and order;
and the religion of every village in England was forcibly
braced by their arrival. All over the country new
churches were built, and that on a scale hitherto unknown; to this day no buildings are so impressive in

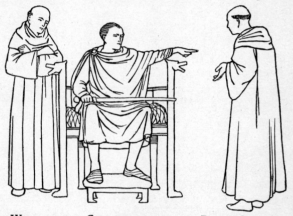

WILLIAM THE CONQUEROR AND THE POPE'S LEGATE.

their massy grandeur as those products of Norman architecture (c. 1066–1200) which still abound in England.
It was an important age too for the Papacy; the mighty
Hildebrand was raising the Roman see to a height never
attained before; and in England the influx of foreign
clergy brought the Church into closer connection with
the Pope and increased his supremacy. None the less
William the Conqueror, though he had landed with the
Pope's blessing, was not the man to yield his own rights.
When the legate demanded that William should do
homage to the Pope and pay up the arrears of Peter's
Pence, the King answered, "To do homage I refuse,

because I never promised to do it, nor do I find that
my predecessors have ever done it. As for the money,
it shall be more regularly paid." And the King "exer-
cised without question or remonstrance a supremacy
over all persons, ecclesiastical as well as civil, within his
dominions, as real as any enjoyed by Henry VIII or
Elizabeth." [1]

Yet the Papal influence definitely grew ; William
was on the best terms with the Pope : the Norman
bishops had grown accustomed to regard Rome as the
great central authority of the Church. The Church
courts were separated from the civil, and this meant the
adoption of a system of canon law. The Normans
also spread the feudal system, by which every man
had a master.[2] In theology, the doctrine of tran- 1050–79
substantiation was just arising out of the Berengarian 1076
controversy. Clerical celibacy was ordered through
Hildebrand's influence by Lanfranc in the Council of
Winchester.

Monasticism

New convents arose everywhere, and monasticism
was the order of the day : all men valued the holy
presence and prayers of the monks, and a Norman
baron who did not endow or found a monastery would
have been looked down upon at least as much as a
modern peer who gave nothing in charity to the
hospitals or the poor. And monasticism responded to
the call : new and still severer communities were   1077

[1] H. O. Wakeman, *History of the Church of England*, 3rd ed. (1897),
p. 93.
[2] The centralizing policy of Rome also produced, alas ! the schism
with the Eastern Church (1098), which has not yet been healed.

founded in England, the Cluniacs being the model
1028 order. They were followed fifty years later by the
Cistercians, another body of reformed Benedictines,
whose life was yet harder, and their services of puritan
simplicity, with plain linen altar-cloths, censers of iron,
and one iron candlestick for the altar : yet they built
the glorious abbeys of Rievaulx, Fountains, Kirkstall,
and Tintern.

1105 There were also brought to England in the 12th
century the Austin or " Black" Canons, and another order
of canons who lived a monastic life, the "White" Canons.
1143 But the latest order of monks was the sternest of all, the
1180 Carthusians, whose first prior was the brave and tender
Hugh of Avalon, known later as St. Hugh of Lincoln.
At a Charterhouse each monk lived in a separate cell,
and only spoke on Sundays and festivals : they never ate
meat : cheese was a rare luxury, and they fasted one day
a week on bread and water. All monks rose at midnight
to say Mattins and Lauds, and at daybreak rose again for
Prime and Mass ; then came the chapter-meeting, Terce,
High Mass, Sext. Not till after that was the first meal
of the day ; then work of various kinds, then None,
more work and recreation, Evensong, supper, reading,
Compline, and then bed till midnight struck again. They
cultivated the land and built, they wrote and illuminated
books in the chilly cloister, they managed schools and
hospitals, gave hospitality to travellers, and succoured
the poor and outcast.

In a short history like this we may not linger over
many beautiful lives and noble deeds. St. Anselm was
the greatest genius of his age, a theologian who ranks
with the earlier Fathers, and was foremost for his love
and goodness, in an age of saints. He succeeded Lanfranc

as Prior of Bec in 1063, and Herluin as Abbot in 1078. The terrible Conqueror himself became mild in his presence, and when dying sought his blessing ; but **1093** after St. Anselm was made Archbishop of Canterbury, he had to endure a long struggle with King William Rufus, whose iniquities and sacrilegious rapacity he bravely rebuked and withstood.

LATE NORMAN ARCHITECTURE: BILDWAS ABBEY.

Even the **1095** Crusades, of which the first was in 1095, need only be mentioned here. They illustrate the growth of martial chivalry; they ultimately brought us many good things from the East, where, by the way, the Crusaders first heard about St. George. They affected English life in many ways. But they were on the whole a disastrous failure, fulfilling nothing of their noble projects.

St. Thomas à Becket

In the next century there took place a struggle between Church and State which provided England with her most popular saint for the rest of the Middle Ages.

There was right on both sides in that titanic conflict between Henry II and Thomas Becket, Archbishop of Canterbury. On the one hand Henry, in his great work of bringing orderly government into the chaos left by King Stephen, was right in not letting the clergy slip outside the national system. The Constitutions of Clarendon were " really a part of a great scheme of administrative reform," and not a mere weapon of spite.[1] On the other hand, Thomas was right to resist the royal dictatorship in the name of the Church. He did so in the cause of clerical privilege ; but " Freedom decked herself with the plumes of privilege to hide her true character from the searching eyes of despotic power."[2]

1164

A BISHOP,
c. 1170.

The popular instinct saw this. " Religion grew more and more identified with patriotism,"[3] and the heroic stand of Becket against the strong and terrible King laid the foundations for the free, united England that was to emerge. The people adored the memory of St. Thomas, because, when every liberty was in danger of destruction by the King's officials, the archbishop had stood out inflexible,

[1] Bishop Stubbs, *Constitutional History of England*, vol. i, pp. 465-6. The Constitutions of Clarendon lay it down, among other matters, that clergy accused of crime should not be protected by the Church against the King's courts ; that appeals were to go from archdeacon to bishop, from bishop to archbishop, but not farther (i.e. to the Pope) without the King's leave.

[2] H. O. Wakeman, *History of the Church of England*, 3rd ed. (1897), p. 108.

[3] J. R. Green, *Short History*, cap. ii, sec. viii.

and in his own solitary person had dammed the tide that
threatened to sweep liberty away.   For this he died.

On a winter evening at Canterbury, the cry arose,
" Armed men in the cloister ! "   Four knights, shouting
" King's men ! King's men ! " followed Becket, as, re-

THE MURDER OF ST. THOMAS A BECKET.—By G. E. Kruger-Gray.

fusing to escape, he walked up from the cloister to the
choir.   They fell on him in the transept, and there cut
him down with their swords and foully murdered him.
All Europe was horrified.   Soon Henry himself was
kneeling in penance at his shrine ; and thenceforward   **1174**

that shrine was the favourite centre of pilgrimages, and St. Thomas of Canterbury the darling of England till another Henry and a more ruthless autocrat swept the shrine away, and removed from the English Kalendar the name of the saint who had withstood a king in the day of his wrath.[1] St. Anselm had done it before ; Stephen Langton was soon to do it again at Runnymede, where the hard-won liberties of England were finally established.

Magna Carta, 1215

Magna Carta fixed for ever what had before been vague and shadowy, and became the pivot of all future

MAGNA CARTA: THE BISHOPS AND BARONS BEFORE KING JOHN AT RUNNYMEDE.—By G. E. Kruger-Gray.

[1] Henry VIII in 1538.

constitutional government. Archbishop Stephen Langton
was the statesman who guided the barons to this policy.
The people chafed at the royal tyranny, but knew not
what they wanted.
The archbishop
saw that the root
of the evil was
that the King's
will was above
the law, and the
principle of free-
dom still unde-
fined. Once more
the Church of
England led the
way in the struggle
for freedom.
King John reluct-
antly granted the
Charter, after his
humiliation under
that Pope who
raised the power
of Rome to the
highest point it
ever attained.[1]

THE CRYPT: CANTERBURY CATHEDRAL.
c. 1220.

[1] Innocent III
(1198-1216), whose
rule marks the high-
water mark of the Papacy. The disgrace of Boniface VIII at Anagni
in 1303 is called by Creighton "the Fall of the Mediaeval Papacy."
The next downward step was the "Babylonish Captivity" of the
Popes at Avignon (1305-67); then followed the "Great Schism,"
1378-1414. In 1517 Luther began the Reformation, since which

Langton was present, and Hubert de Burgh, and the Mayor of London, and the barons :

"The Church of England shall be free, her privileges respected, her right to free election not infringed upon." "It shall be so."
"To no man shall be sold, or denied, or delayed right or justice." "The King wills it."

Thus the archbishop and the barons saved England from royal and papal tyranny by one stroke. John, after much defiance, had grovelled to the Papacy as no other king ever did before or since ; he had agreed to hold England and Ireland as fiefs of the Pope, and to pay an annual tribute for them. After the Charter had been signed, Innocent III had the audacity to cancel it, to "excommunicate the barons by name and in the lump," and to suspend Stephen Langton from his archbishopric. Needless to say these measures were futile.

The Thirteenth Century

This was in the 13th century, the greatest, as many think, of all centuries, the age of St. Francis and St. Dominic, of St. Thomas Aquinas, St. Bonaventura, Innocent III, Albertus Magnus, St. Louis, Cimabue, Giotto, Nicolò Pisano, and of most of Dante's life ; the age when the continental nations were created, and parliaments began, and the Universities of Paris and Oxford ; the age when science dawned, and the telescope was invented, and gunpowder ; in England the age of Roger Bacon, and of the great schoolmen Duns Scotus,

the decline of papal power has continued, so that at the present day the papal claims are repudiated by the Governments even of Roman Catholic countries like Italy and France.

Alexander Hales, William of Ockham, of Edward I, the greatest of our lawgivers, and also of Bishop Grosseteste and St. Hugh of Lincoln. The last name reminds us that the 13th century also saw the full flower of Gothic architecture—witness such triumphs of religious beauty as the Sainte-Chapelle in Paris, the cathedral at Amiens; in England St. Hugh's own cathedral of Lincoln, Salisbury Cathedral, the most typical example of "Early English" architecture, and a host of other glorious churches which are still the noblest visible things in our land, and by which, more than by aught else, the Middle Ages are known to the men of to-day.

EARLY ENGLISH ARCHITECTURE: LINCOLN MINSTER.

The Coming of the Friars

This was the century too in which the Friars came to England. They were founded by the two saints just

THE COMING OF THE FRIARS.

By C. O. Skilbeck.

mentioned, the Italian St. Francis of Assisi and the † 1226
Spaniard St. Dominic. St. Francis was perhaps the † 1221
most Christlike man who ever lived, and no saint is
more loved at the present day : his influence over
Europe was immense. He in fact regenerated Western
Christendom. The followers of St. Francis were called
Franciscans or Grey Friars from the colour of their
habits ; those of St. Dominic, the Dominicans, wore
black and white and were called Black Friars, whence
in London to-day we have Blackfriars Bridge. The
Friars, i.e. *frères*, 'brothers,' represented a further
reform of monasticism : they were not only to have
no private property, but were to have nothing at all
except shelter and the rough gown and hood of a
peasant ; barefooted and bareheaded they were to go,
and to live on the bread they could beg from the
charitable. The first Dominicans landed in England 1221
soon after Magna Carta, and were welcomed by Stephen
Langton. The first Franciscans came three years later ; 1224
a little band of nine men, they asked for the coarsest
fare and the meanest lodging, and then began their
work. Into the hovels and slums the Franciscans went,
in every part of England, lodging with the outcasts
and lepers beyond the city gates. They lived Christ,
and brought Christ everywhere, these mighty street
preachers, who made fellowship with the miserable, and
lit up Europe with their Gospel-message.

In spite of themselves the Friars soon produced
great scholars—Alexander Hales, Duns Scotus, Peckham
who became Archbishop of Canterbury, William of
Ockham, "the Invincible Doctor," and, greatest of
all, the ill-treated Roger Bacon, precursor of modern
science. These were Franciscans, as was also "the

F

Seraphic Doctor," St. Bonaventura.   Albertus Magnus,
" the Universal Doctor," and St. Thomas Aquinas,
" the Angelical Doctor," were both Dominicans.   The
Friars also became
rich and powerful,
as St. Francis had
dreaded they might :
they built great
churches and houses.
They undoubtedly
fell away from their
first ideal ; but their
decline in the 14th
and 15th centuries
has been much
exaggerated : they
continued to be " the
friends of the poor
and the evangelizers
of the masses," and
they were entirely
supported by volun-
tary contributions.

ALEXANDER HALES RECEIVING HOLY
COMMUNION.
(From a contemporary MS.)

Their begging life did indeed attract many vagabonds,
and whatever evil was done by such men was naturally
open and notorious.   But we know that in the awful
plague of 1348–9, called the Black Death, thousands
of Friars died at their post ; and the leaders of the
Peasant Revolt under Wat Tyler, in 1381, always spared
the Friars, who, they said, would be the peoples' guides
to heaven when all the machinery of the Church was
done away with.

CHAPTER 9

THE STRUGGLE WITH THE PAPACY

FROM the days of the great Hildebrand the influence of the Papacy grew enormously. We must not make the mistake of supposing that this growth was the result merely of papal pretensions unceasingly presented to the world. It was rather because the world needed in those days such a power. We must always remember that it was the best popes that made the Papacy, and not the worst. Thus Gregory the Great, who in an earlier day had indignantly refused the title of Universal Bishop, did more for the Papacy than any one of his predecessors had done.

Why did the world need the Papacy, then? Chiefly as a rallying point around which men could gather to resist the secularizing influences of the great lay lords. There were many men who lived as Rufus had done; and the only power that could deal with them was the Church. The Investiture Controversy is an illustration of this. Laymen claimed the power of conferring spiritual character. If this claim had been acknowledged, then the great Church offices would have been filled often by the creatures of unworthy nobles. But Churchmen only succeeded in refusing this claim by drawing closer together under one leader, and so presenting a united front to the world.

This work of closing-up the ranks was greatly aided by the Cluniacs, who from the first preached everywhere "high" doctrine, and who numbered amongst their ranks the great Hildebrand himself. Anxious, from the highest motives, to hasten on this centralizing movement, the Papacy lent too ready an ear to certain documents which are now known to be forgeries, viz. the *Donation of Constantine* and the *Decretals*.[1] A tremendous deal also was made of the fact that St. Peter had been Bishop of Rome. It was asserted that St. Peter had had an authority superior to that of the other Apostles, and that this superiority had descended by inheritance to the successive occupants of the "Chair of St. Peter." Furthermore, to prevent national Churches from taking an independent line, the popes used to send out legates who, as representing the Papacy, claimed authority over all local archbishops or bishops.

In 1126 the Archbishop of Canterbury accepted the Legateship for England, and by so doing acknowledged the Supremacy of the Papacy over the English Church.

But then came long years when the holders of the Papacy were seen more and more to be unworthy of their great office, until at last, towards the end of the 13th century, the whole theory of the Papacy was attacked.

Ockham and Marsiglio

St. Thomas Aquinas had accepted without question the mediaeval western theory of the Papacy ; but, about

1274 the year of his death, was born William of Ockham, "The Invincible Doctor," who not only attacked with

1325 his trenchant pen the corruption of the Papacy—which was the result of that worldliness and wealth which the

---

[1] The Forged Donation, which represents Constantine as bestowing Italy and the West on the Pope, belongs to the 8th century. The False Decretals, purporting to begin in the 1st century, are also not earlier than the 8th.

Franciscans of that time specially disliked because of their Gospel of Poverty—but also attacked its claims to temporal monarchy and spiritual infallibility.[1] About the same time, an Italian, greater even than the English Franciscan Ockham, went to the heart of the matter

Briar.

and exposed the rottenness of the beams upon which the whole Papal supremacy rested. This was Marsiglio of Padua, whose *Defensor Pacis* revolutionized the thought of Latin Christendom: it was the great storehouse for the writers of the 14th and 15th centuries —that is, until Luther; and for a century and a half after its publication no books were written in defence of the Papal power.

1327

Pricking the Bubble

Marsiglio pricked the mediaeval bubble. He pointed out that St. Peter had no authority over the other Apostles; that the appointment of ecclesiastics rests not with the Pope but with the community of the faithful, as is shown by the appointment of the first deacons in Acts vi. 2–6; that the Catholic Faith is one, and rests on Scripture only, but when any doubts arise they are to be settled by a general

[1] M. Creighton, *History of the Papacy*, vol. i, p. 36.

council of the faithful, in which laity and clergy alike have seats; and that the Roman bishop, though he should act as president of such councils, could have no power of coercion, of interdict, or excommunication beyond what the council might choose to confer.

This book of Marsiglio, the first example of the modern scientific method, began the Reformation. It appeared fifty years before Wycliffe, so that we must not allow our national prejudice to make us suppose that Wycliffe was the real founder of the Reformation: as a matter of fact Wycliffe, by his wild theories, did much to promote the reaction against reforming ideas in the 15th century. People talk about Wycliffe a great deal without dreaming of reading him: his involved scholastic arguments would be fatal to any idea of good government, whether modern or ancient; and he is not to be compared with Marsiglio, who recovered the ancient Church idea of constitutional government, and taught his age the principles on which the Anglican and the Orthodox Eastern Churches rest to-day—the principles of Catholic order.[1]

A PRIEST IN SURPLICE, ALMUCE, AND CLOTH COPE.

The system of the Early Church was a federation of local Churches, with an appeal to the General Council of the whole Church. This has never ceased to be the system of the Orthodox Church of the East. It is also the system of the Anglican Church to-day. The

[1] There is an interesting comparison of Marsiglio and Wycliffe in Creighton's *History of the Papacy*, vol. i, pp. 104-5.

system of the Roman Church has become a despotism. It was this despotism that Marsiglio exposed, and he appealed to the Catholic practice of a General Council of the whole Church. Time has shown that he was right; for despotisms have had their day.

Papal Exactions

The people and Parliament of England did not at first trouble their heads with these great principles; but they were very much concerned with the practical side of the matter, for

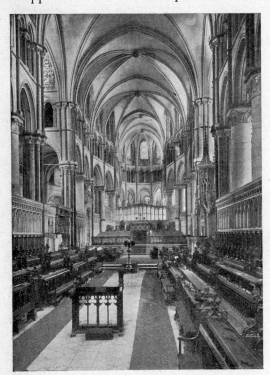

CANTERBURY CATHEDRAL: THE CHOIR.
(Begun after the fire of 1172.)

Papal exactions became intolerable in the 13th century. After Magna Carta and the death of King John, there **1216-72** "ruled" for fifty-six years the weak and needy Henry III, who described himself (following King John) as the feudatory of the Pope. The King's exactions during this dreary reign led to the growth of constitutionalism, in the great struggle of Simon de Montfort, whose trusted friend and adviser was the brave and learned Grosseteste, Bishop of Lincoln. The King's weakness led also to the Pope's barefaced encroachments.

† 1253

The Pope extorted incredible sums of money, and appointed his Italian friends to the richest posts in the Church.[1] He sent the notorious Otho to demand one prebend of every cathedral, and an equivalent income from every bishop, for the popes for ever. This was refused; but four years later the Pope got one-tenth of all clerical property in England —an income tax of 2*s.* in the pound! Then he demanded *one-fifth* of all the English bishops' revenues, and 300 English benefices. Next came the Nuncio Martin, who behaved with intolerable arrogance and demanded *one-third* of all English benefices—an income-tax of 6*s.* 8*d.* in the pound—for three years. This was too much.

1225

1229

1240

SIMON DE MONTFORT.

[1] Pandulph, the legate, was "bishop" of Norwich—that is to say, he enjoyed the revenue of the see—for seven years before he was even consecrated a bishop. During Henry III's reign, in Salisbury alone, 6 deans, 3 precentors, 2 chancellors, and 9 canons or prebendaries were appointed by the Pope. The foreigners drew 60,000 marks annually—more than the whole revenue of the King.

The Great Council sent Martin a solemn warning that if he and his colleagues wished to keep a whole bone in their bodies they had better leave the country at once. Even the royal worm seems to have turned; for Matthew Paris tells us that he heard Henry say, when Martin asked for a safe-conduct out of England—"May the devil conduct you to the infernal regions!"

The Church and English Liberty

Now, the real result of King Henry III's misgovernment was the development of English nationality in opposition to King and Pope alike. Constitutionalism was established; and once more it was the English Church that secured the liberties of England :

> "The mitre," says Sir Francis Palgrave, "has resisted many blows which would have broken the helmet. . . . It is to these prelates that we chiefly owe the maintenance of the form and the spirit of free government, secured to us not by force but by law; and the altar has thus been the cornerstone of our ancient constitution."

Edward I

A BISHOP: 14TH CENTURY.

Edward I, "the greatest of the Plantagenets," completed the constitutional work, by his great fundamental laws, by his organization of the law-courts, by his perfecting of the parliamentary system. England had become able to fend for herself. But under the misrule of Edward II

1272-1307

1307-27 abuses grew up, society was demoralized, the bishops were on the whole of low repute and unpopular : the age of great men was over. 1327-77 This condition continued under Edward III ; but during his reign certain things happened which greatly affected the future of the Church.

The "Babylonish Captivity"

1338
1453
The Hundred Years' War with France began under Edward III.

THE LAST MARCH OF EDWARD I.—By William Bell Scott.

This increased the national opposition to the popes, since they were now Frenchmen, puppets of the French **1305–77** King, and exiles from Rome, in their "Babylonish Captivity" at Avignon.   No sooner had the Papacy got back to Rome than the Great Papal Schism **1378–** began, during **1414** which there were two and sometimes three popes —a scandal which set men thinking.

DECORATED GOTHIC: THE LADY CHAPEL OF WELLS CATHEDRAL.

The Black Death

Meanwhile the **1349** horrible plague, called the Black Death, swept over Europe. The clergy, monks, and friars behaved splendidly, and died at their posts.[1] But their places had to be filled by the ordaining of inferior men, and even then many parishes were for long without a priest.   At the same time the

---

[1] In East Anglia, in one single year, over 800 parishes lost their parsons ; in 83 of these the successor died as well ; in 10 the third priest also died within the year.

monasteries were so crippled in numbers and efficiency that they never recovered : worst of all their schools trained fewer men for Holy Orders. Their discipline became lax; for their vast buildings had much money and few men in them, and idleness crept on. The monks built no more great abbeys. Monasticism never recovered from the double evil of accumulated wealth and decay in numbers ; and so it was the easier destroyed, first here and there by the founding of colleges, as we shall see, and finally in 1539.

AFTER THE BLACK DEATH : PERPENDICULAR GOTHIC.

The age of activity and progress was passed ; an age of reduced efficiency and much discontent had begun.

Churches indeed were built after the Black Death ; but during that awful period architecture had stopped. The Decorated style died. When Church building began again after the Black Death, it was in a new style —that which is called Perpendicular. The abundance of this, the only architecture which is of our own invention and peculiar to England, shows how much building was done from now till the reign of Henry VIII. The abundance of chantry chapels in the Perpendicular style also illustrates the curious change in religion that followed the Black Death: it became more subdued and introspective; men thought more about the dead and about death, and gave themselves to new devotions, such as those of the Holy Name, or the Five Wounds, and to an intensified veneration of the saints.

A DIRGE: CHANTERS SINGING ROUND HEARSE, WITH ALTAR IN THE DISTANCE.
(From a 15th century MS.)

A LAYMAN: 14TH CENTURY.

Anti-Papal Laws

It was not a good time for the popes to continue their encroachments. None the less, they did so. Especially they claimed more and more the right to enrich their friends with English benefices; ever since Henry III's weak reign they had been struggling for the power of patronage in England. But the nation rose, and Parliament passed the famous Statutes of *Provisors* and *Praemunire*.

1351, 1353

The Statute of *Provisors* (1351, re-enacted in 1390) enacted that the Pope should not in future appoint to any bishoprics or benefices in

England. The Statute of *Praemunire* (1353, re-enacted in 1365 and 1393) forbade any person to bring papal bulls or letters into England without the King's leave, under penalty of imprisonment and forfeiture of goods ; it declared the same penalty against any person who should carry into the papal court any case over which the royal courts had lawful jurisdiction.

John Wycliffe

Then, with these anti-papal Acts already on the Statute Book, with the writings of Ockham and Marsiglio familiar to all the scholars of Europe, there arose a more famous disciple of Ockham in the person of John Wycliffe, who began to attack the papal theory about 1373.

c. 1324– 84

Every age has its virtues and its faults, and each generation is quick at discerning the faults of another. Certainly there were " sins, negligences, and ignorances " in the Middle Ages ; and the name of Wycliffe means to most Englishmen the dawn of the Reformation, though indeed he was the last of the Schoolmen rather than the first of the Reformers. He withstood the Pope (there were two of them at the time), and called him " the head vicar of the fiend " ; indeed he called most ecclesiastics devils of some sort, including the English bishops, who were " horned fiends to be damned in hell." This mastery of language made him very popular at Oxford. He was also learned, with an intimate knowledge of the Bible. But he went further than his predecessors, and boldly attacked the sacramental teaching of the time. He affirmed indeed the Real Presence of Christ in the Eucharist ; but he poured utter scorn on the philosophic idea of Transubstantiation, to deny which was then considered a terrible heresy.

Wycliffe met with much bitter opposition ; but he withstood it in the spirit of a splendid, indomitable

Wycliffe sending out his Poor Preachers.—By W. F. Yeames.

Englishman — pouring out numberless controversial tracts that were written in mordant English or Latin, and sending out "Poor Preachers" who were modelled on those of St. Francis. And though he was tried more than once, he had powerful friends; and after having raised up a host of disciples, he died peacefully while saying Mass at Lutterworth in 1384. Most of all, he completed the work of Bede and later scholars by translat-

INITIAL LETTER FROM A WYCLIFFE BIBLE, SHOWING A "JESSE" TREE.

ing the Bible in full, and giving to England the first of those various English Bibles, the noblest monuments of the piety and learning of the English Church. Already there was, indeed, a translation of the whole Bible in the Court French which the educated classes spoke ; but Wycliffe translated it into the " vulgar tongue."

A PILGRIM ✝
14ᵗ CENTURY

CHAPTER 10

THE FIFTEENTH CENTURY

WYCLIFFE'S followers, the Lollards, soon became
lost amongst the great number of people whose
aim was social revolution. It was this political aspect

CHURCH BUILDING. (From a 15th century MS.)

of things that gave rise to the severe laws against
heresy which now defiled the Statute Book, and, from
the Statute *De Heretico Comburendo*, in 1401, added a
new horror to English life. At first, then, the Lollards
were punished rather as disturbers of the peace than as

teachers of false doctrine. And so, because Lollardism had become political, it died down rapidly all over the England of the 15th century.

This age saw the final culmination of Gothic architecture, and a wonderful growth of art all over Europe ;

but religious enthusiasm slept. The Church seemed to be stationary, but she was really slipping back. She was still the Church of the people ; but she no longer led the people. The abuses which Wycliffe had tried to stop grew worse. The Papacy had sunk to a scheming Italian princedom ; the Papal Court was a byword for corruption.

"The night is darkest before the dawn." [1] At least in the Christian Era there is always recovery in the midst of dissolution. The 15th century did after all produce that adorable wonder Joan of Arc, and great men, like the Frenchmen d'Ailly and Gerson, who would have reformed the Church had they been given the chance ; and it

A KNIGHT:
c. 1450.

is cheering to reflect that among the miseries and disasters of that age the *Imitation of Christ* was written, probably by an Englishman. Only, the great men did not hold great positions ; and this shows the character of the age as a whole.

[1] Certainly one of the darkest days in Christian history was that in 1453, when Constantinople, the splendid centre of Eastern Christendom, fell into the hands of the Turks. The Hundred Years' War spluttered out to its inglorious close in the same year ; and two years later the wicked and disastrous Wars of the Roses had begun.

To all ages God's good men have been given; but the spirit of some ages has kept such men in the background. Norman England loved its saints, and set them up to rule; therefore the Norman period was great. But men of the 15th century preferred aristocrats to saints; and the bishoprics were mainly given to members of those families whose fierce, unscrupulous selfishness tore England to pieces, and finally accomplished their own destruction in the Wars of the Roses. These wars indeed decimated the English nobility.

Courtier 14ᵗʰ Century.

But if we think mainly of the *people* we shall find the old Church life going on pretty much as before. Let us look at it as it was until the tyrants of the 16th century broke it up under pretence of theological reform.

The Religion of Old England

Abuses generally fasten upon the prominent and richly endowed offices. Everybody in those days was a Churchman; and thus many worldly and wicked men sought the rich revenues and important positions that belonged to the Church—many too who in our day would be politicians, with a politician's standard of

"UNSCRUPULOUS LAWYERS" OF THE 15TH CENTURY.

consistency and disinterestedness. The affairs of the Church were also largely in the hands of unscrupulous lawyers ; and it is to the ecclesiastical lawyers that the exactions and injustices of the age were mainly due.

The Parson

But beneath all this, the ordinary parish priest of small means lived his ordinary life, and did his duty ; very constant in the services of his church, visiting the sick, diligently catechizing in the Creed, the Lord's Prayer, and the Ten Commandments, teaching the peasant lads, and (by means of the monasteries) sending the brightest of them to Oxford or Cambridge. Chaucer, who held up so many of his characters to ridicule in the *Canterbury Tales*, had nothing but praise for the village parson — whom he so beautifully describes :

CHAUCER'S PARSON.
(From the Ellesmere MS.)

"A good man there was of relig'ioun,
That was a poorè parson of a toun [1];
But richè was of holy thought and work.
He was alsó a learnèd man, a clerk,
That Christè's Gospel truèly would preach.
His parishens [2] devoutly would he teach.
Benigne he was, and wonder [3] diligent,
And in adversity full patïent;
And such he was yprovèd often, sithes [4]
Full loth were he to cursen [5] for his tithes,
But rather would he given, out of doubt, [6]
Unto his poorè parishens about,
Of his offèring, and eke of his substánce,
He could in little thing have suffisance.
Wide was his parish, and houses far asunder,
But he ne left nought, for no rain ne thunder,
In sickness and in mischief [7] to visit
The farthest in his parish much and lite, [8]
Upon his feet, and in his hand a staff.
This noble example to his sheep he gave
That first he wrought and afterward he taught:
Out of the Gospel he the wordès caught;
And this figúre he added yet thereto,
That if gold rustè, what should iron do?"

Or, as we might say, Rusty priests make rotten people—a
truth which was sadly exemplified in later days. Chaucer
concludes his long description with the famous couplet—

"But Christè's lore, and his Apostles twelve,
He taught, but first he followed it himself."

The People

And what are we to say of the parson's flock? They
were sturdy Englishmen, comfortably off in those days,

[1] *toun*, town or village.   [2] *parishens*, parishioners.
[3] *wonder*, wonderfully.   [4] *sithes*, since.
[5] *to cursen*, to curse or upbraid.   [6] *out of doubt*, without doubt.
[7] *mischief*, trouble.   [8] *much and lite*, great and small.

and as yet unsoured by Puritanism, though they
endured many hardships and approved many cruelties.
For there seems to be no doubt that the phrase
"Merrie England" was not undeserved : they had
more of that outdoor life and free geniality which we

A MIRACLE PLAY IN THE 14TH CENTURY.—By C. O. Skilbeck.

now associate with France, and they enjoyed a large
number of play-days, since all the Holy Days were
really holidays, till the Tudors abolished them. Our
present "Bank" Holidays are a poor substitute for
the crowd of festivals which the people once had.
These holidays, like everything else, centred round the
Church, and were not called after banks. Englishmen
then had religion in the blood, and all belonged to

one communion and fellowship; indeed to be cut off from the Church by excommunication was the most terrible of penalties.

There was more violence and passion, no doubt; but also there was more repentance. The worst men belonged still to the Church, recognized a standard above their own, and often repented as violently as they had sinned. The religion of those times had many limitations, and in many ways we should find it insufficient to-day; but every one knew what his duty

PILGRIMS.
(From a late 15th century MS.)

was, and how to do it. The heritage of bitterness and misunderstanding which is ours to-day—the confusion of wrangling sects, the vast mass of religious ignorance and indifference—these did not then exist. All Englishmen were Churchmen, and they worshipped the same Master in the same way, young and old, rich and poor, one with another; for the Church belonged to all classes alike—the brother of Chaucer's parson was a ploughman—

> "An honest labourer, and a good was he,
> Living in peace and perfect charity."

These men of England loved their parish churches. We have those noble buildings still all over England to-

AN OUTDOOR PROCESSION.
(From a 15th century MS.)

day, though they are now but the cold shadows of what they once were. Into those churches the people poured their treasures ; in the ever-varying festivals of those churches they found their great delight. In every village of England there stood a church, built generally by the parishioners themselves, the matchless carving worked by local carpenters and masons—built mainly at the people's expense and owned by them ; for the churches belonged to the parishioners, and not to the parson.

The extent of the popular demand for the ministrations of the Gospel may be imagined from the supply. At the time of the Norman Conquest England, with a population of only about two millions, had about 20 dioceses and 8,000 parishes. If we had kept up the proportion to-day London alone would now have some 50 bishops and, say, 20,000 parish churches ! It is said that in Plantagenet London there was a parish church in every street. A return of 1516, enumerates

168 houses of God in London, of which 113 were parish churches within the city itself. York, in the reign of Henry V (with a population of only about 11,000) had 41 parish churches, with a large number of chapels as well; and the number of clergy, both regular and secular, was not less than 500. Norwich had 25 churches in Anglo-Saxon times, 54 (including chapels) in the Domesday Book, 45 at the end of the 13th century, and just before the Reformation there were 37 vicarages, besides chapels and the cathedral.

And in the villages, as in the towns, the people had their guilds—trade-unions which not only maintained the standard of work, wages and prices very rigidly, but also cared for the sick, and prayed for the dead, often having their own chapel or altar in the church. It was the wealth of these guilds, their gold and silver plate for village feasts, together with the treasure of the parish churches, the superb chalices and pyxes and crosses and banners and vestments, that tempted the cupidity of the robbers in Edward VI's reign. Luckily for the historian those same robbers caused inventories to be made, which are being

A LADY OF THE 14TH CENTURY.

printed and published to-day, so that we can now form an idea of the people's church treasures.

On Sundays and Holy Days the people went to Mattins, Mass, and Evensong, just as Church people do now—and, alas, that "Church people" no longer

means " *the* people." Perhaps it is worth while men-
tioning, since old prejudices still exist, that by " Mass "
our forefathers meant the Holy Communion. There are
many still who imagine (never having opened a missal)
that the Latin Mass is a corrupt and superstitious
service invented in the Middle Ages : as a matter of
fact it is a Communion Service of very sober and re-
strained language, the bulk of which belongs to the 6th
century. So too with Mattins and Evensong : our modern
services

A Bishop celebrating the Lord's Supper
before a King.

(From a 15th century MS.)

(with the more simple and dignified of our modern
hymns) are but condensed translations of those used
in the Middle Ages.

These services were for the most part in Latin. But
even here fairness obliges us to admit that the common
people loved and understood the services when they
were in Latin better than they do now that they are in

English.   It is a sad confession, for our noble English services ought to be far more intelligible ; but the reason is that the parsons of those days were exceedingly diligent teachers, whereas *our* parsons are only now re- viving the work of catechizing ; and also they had a willing and loving people to teach.   Moreover in those days Latin was much more generally known : it was the language, not only of all scholars, but even of bailiffs, land-agents, clerks, and such-like people.   The Bidding Prayer was, of course, in English, and was very popular for that reason.   There was a good deal of preaching, many books of devotion, and a not inconsiderable amount of English translations of the Bible in the 15th century.   But, as printing was not invented till near the end of that century, the possibility of diffusing sacred books widely had not arisen.

GILBERTINE CANON.

There were evils and abuses.   Though people loved to go to Mass, most men only communicated once a year.   The practice too of the people communicating in one kind only had become general,[1] and in 1415 it was made into a law.   Enforced clerical celibacy also was an evil ; for it narrowed the ecclesiastical mind, and the fact that many priests (and popes, and high ecclesiastics like Cardinal Wolsey) evaded it

[1] This practice had arisen because men grew their hair on their faces in such an unkempt fashion that it was difficult for them to receive from the chalice without irreverence.

had a bad moral effect. There were also other evils of prelacy and popery, which are mentioned in this history.

Then came a great upheaval of European thought, the Renaissance. A change was necessary ; reform was needed. But how much happier would it have been for Christendom if both sides in the huge battle of the Reformation had shown a Christian spirit, and reform had come in a better way !

CHAPTER 11

THE RENAISSANCE AND REFORMATION

IMMEASURABLY the most important of the 15th century movements was the revival of learning. This is illustrated by the founding of the many colleges that were dedicated to religion and education between 1382 and 1525. For, above all things, the 15th century was the supreme period of the Renaissance, which, indeed, largely took a pagan form on the Continent, but was Christian in England, where ecclesiastical abuses and the consequent reaction were less.

HENRY VI AS A BOY PRESENTED TO THE BLESSED VIRGIN.
(From a contemporary picture.)

1422-71 King Henry VI was a perfect patron of letters—saintly and studious, generous, simple, merciful, just—and therefore unfitted for his turbulent and selfish times. To London alone he gave nine

94

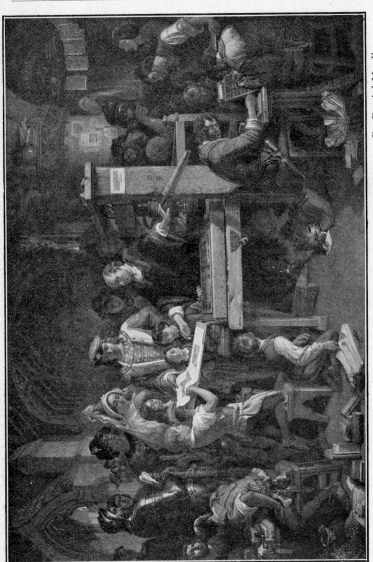

Edward IV visiting Caxton's Printing Press at Westminster.—By Daniel Maclise.

grammar schools. He founded the University of Caen before he was twelve years old, established Eton College at eighteen, and by the time he was twenty-six had finished King's College at Cambridge. Certainly a dead era could neither have reared these noble centres of learning, nor filled England with the magnificent churches that were built or rebuilt in the 15th century.

1455-71 The Wars of the Roses

ARCHBISHOP WARHAM.
(After Holbein.)

stopped such gracious work. But when they were over, the New Learning burst out and the century closed in a blaze of light. Caxton was busy with his printing press, which he had started in 1476. Henry VII's first

1486

SIR THOMAS MORE.
(After Holbein.)
Lord Chancellor of England, author of the *Utopia*. Conspicuous all his life in the cause of Church Reform, he opposed Henry VIII's assumption of supremacy over the Church, and was beheaded in 1535.

chancellor, Cardinal Morton ; and Warham, who after two years succeeded him as Archbishop of Canterbury ; Cardinal Wolsey, Archbishop of York, who got the chancellorship from Warham ; and Sir Thomas

1503

1515

1529 More, who was chancellor after Wolsey's fall—all these carried on the tradition that the greatest statesmen and ecclesiastics should patronize the Humanist movement, which, by regenerating scholarship and science, was taking men back to the Bible and the Fathers, and thus sapping the scholasticism of the Middle Ages.[1] Already in Henry VII's reign there flourished Grocyn, Colet, Bishop Fox, Linacre, Erasmus, and Sir Thomas More [2]— men who began the Re-formation in the spirit of

BISHOP FOX.
(After a contemporary portrait at Corpus Christi College, Oxford.)

[1] We must be careful, however, to avoid the common error of depreciating the great work which the mediaeval thinkers had done. Dr. Rashdall, after speaking of "the enormous services of scholasticism to human progress," says "Nothing betrays more unfailingly a lack of the historical spirit and the historical temper than a tone of un-discriminating contempt in speaking of

ERASMUS.

the scholastic Philosophy and the scholastic Theology," and proceeds to say that the scholastic ideal is much needed to-day—the ideal of a science that shall present religion in due relation to all other branches of knowledge.—Hastings Rashdall, *Doctrine and Development*, University Sermons (1898), pp. 133, 144.

[2] Grocyn, †1519 ; Colet, †1519 ; Fox, 1528 ; Linacre, †1524 Erasmus, †1536 ; More, †1535.

H

THE TOWER AND LONDON BRIDGE.
(Temp. Henry VII.)

broad-minded tolerance that was soon to be lost on
either side.   But it was their influence and the consequent acceptance by the English Church of the New

Learning that ultimately saved us from the extremes both of Romanism and Calvinism alike.

It was *colleges*, then, that were founded in the 15th century, training places for the working parish clergy—not monasteries ; and this was the case when ecclesiastics made their benefactions, men like William of Wykeham, Bishop of Winchester and Chancellor of England, as early as 1382, or Archbishop Chichele, or pious laymen like King Henry VI. For the day of monasticism was over.

WILLIAM OF WYKEHAM.
(From a later portrait at Winchester.)

The Suppression of the Monasteries, 1536–9

WILLIAM OF WYKEHAM'S FAVOURITE CLERKS.
(From his tomb in Winchester Cathedral.)

Henry VIII **1536** swept them to destruction. The suppression of the smaller monasteries was first taken in hand ; these were those with an income of less than £200 a

1539 year. Three years later came the " forced surrender " of the larger monasteries. The suppression was a tyrannous and greedy act ; yet the monasteries were bound to go sooner or later : some had been already suppressed before Henry's day, and that with papal authority.[1]

They had done an immense work in the past : it was monks who converted Great Britain and Ireland, France, and Germany ; it was monks who had pre-served literature and learning during the long ages of warfare and violence ; it was monks who had turned the wild forests and moors of Europe into peaceful farm-lands. But their day was over. We must not indeed lose our

NUNS IN CHOIR.
(From a 15th century MS.)

sense of proportion in this matter, as so many have done : for two centuries monasticism had been declining, but for

[1] Cardinal Wolsey had thus suppressed forty-two monasteries to found his magnificent College of Christ Church, Oxford, in 1524. But long before this Bishop William of Wykeham had got several alien monastic houses for Winchester College, which he incorporated in 1382. William of Waynflete, who was Bishop of Winchester from 1447 to 1486, had done the same for Magdalen College, Oxford ; and so indeed had the pious Henry VI for Eton and King's Colleges.

some twelve centuries before that it had continued its wonderful history, producing countless multitudes of men and women who made utter sacrifice for Christ's sake, and showing its vitality by astonishing revivals, such as those of the Benedictines, the Cistercians, and the Friars. The charges of moral wickedness which used to be brought against them are now known to have been false. They had indeed become comfortable and worldly; but there were still many learned and good men among the monks, and the Act of 1536 itself gave thanks to God that in the larger houses "religion was right well

MONKS IN CHOIR
(Showing the altar on right.
From a 15th century MS.)

kept and observed." The monks were great landowners; about a third of the land and a third of the tithe now belonged to them, through the benefactions of the past[1]; the officials of a great abbey were practically land-agents,

[1] It has been estimated that of the cultivable land one-fifteenth belonged to the monasteries, and that there were about 8,000 monks, nuns, and friars, and about 80,000 people directly or indirectly dependent on the monasteries out of a population of under 4,000,000.

solicitors, and bailiffs, though rather old-fashioned ones, no doubt. Henry wanted the wealth for himself and his courtiers. He took it without justice and without pity : his vultures swooped upon the spoil, turned out the poor plundered monks and nuns, leaving

SUPPRESSION OF A CONVENT.—BY G. E. Kruger-Gray.

them to live or starve as best they might, even brutally martyring some. The people, who were perhaps the greatest losers of all, rose in a serious rebellion ; their "Pilgrimage of grace" was only suppressed because they dispersed of their own free will, trusting a false promise of the tyrant. The spoil was squandered selfishly and speedily : only a small proportion went to public purposes.

The buildings fell gradually into ruin. It was a wicked waste of national property. What might not have been done for the good of the people with those glorious buildings and that great wealth!

The Reformation Parliament, 1529–36

Already there had come the repudiation of the Pope's authority—a good thing ill done. It was not unpopular.

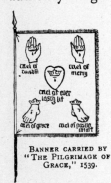

BANNER CARRIED BY "THE PILGRIMAGE OF GRACE," 1539.

The English people as a whole did not indeed desire any theological change; but neither papal exactions nor ecclesiastical abuses were beloved. The Commons welcomed Henry's measures, the Lords unwillingly submitted to them. There was no pretence of justice on the part of the King—still less of mercy. He had told Wolsey to be Papal Legate; then he had the effrontery to charge Wolsey for the crime of having followed his advice and having thus incurred the penalties of *Praemunire*[1]; now, in 1531, he laid the whole clergy of England under *Praemunire* for having accepted Wolsey as Legate! And he made the clergy buy themselves off by paying £100,000 and by acknowledging the grotesque title which the royal robber gave himself of Supreme Head[2] of the Church "as far as the law of Christ allows." The whips of the Papacy were as nothing compared with the scorpions of the King; and though, after a further

[1] See pp. 77–8.
[2] This title disappears from history at the beginning of Elizabeth's reign.

struggle of a hundred years, England made good her freedom against King and Pope alike, the immediate result of Henry's action was that during the rest of his reign he was "King and Pope in one," and "seemed to be making himself almost a god."[1]   All this the King did without even a standing army—with no force indeed except a hundred yeomen of the guard, like those we still see walking about the Tower of London.   The astonishing acquiescence of the nation is doubtless in part to be explained by the fact that the "making-haste to be rich" absorbed the whole faculties of the people[2] ; but it was certainly also due to the destruction of the old nobility in the Wars of the Roses, so that the traditional opponents of royal absolutism had disappeared.

There was as yet no breach of unity in Western Christendom—none indeed till Pius V separated his followers from the English Church in 1570.   Still less is it true that Henry founded a new Church in England : all that was done—by Convocation, Parliament, and the King—was to abolish certain comparatively recent rights of the Pope, and to revive certain long-established and often-exercised rights of the Crown—rights that were now exaggerated and made terribly effective.   In 1534 Convocation passed a resolution that "the Bishop of Rome hath not by Scripture any greater authority in England

A BISHOP.
(Temp. Henry VIII.)

1534

[1] C. R. L. Fletcher, *Introductory History of England* (1907), vol. ii, p. 67.
[2] Ibid. p. 26.

than any other foreign bishop"—a statement undeniably true.   In 1536 an "Act **1536** for extirpating the authority of the Bishop of Rome" was passed by Parliament; by it every layman or ecclesiastic taking office was to take an oath renouncing that bishop.

Meanwhile new ideas were spreading: already in 1521 some of Erasmus's pupils (including Tyndale, Coverdale, and Latimer) were holding secret meetings at Cambridge for the study of Lutheran tracts; Tyndale (in exile) printed his translation of the New Testament in 1525[1]; Coverdale's Bible was issued in

A CANON IN CHOIR.
(Temp. Henry VIII.)

1535 and allowed to circulate; four **1538** years later the Great Bible was issued through the efforts of Cranmer, and ordered to be set up in churches.   The "Bishops' Book" (of instruction in faith and morals) appeared in 1537, the "King's **1544** Book" in 1543.   Next year came the first authorized service in the vulgar tongue: the *Litany* was published in English.

ARCHBISHOP CRANMER.

But Henry VIII held to the old theology; he

[1] It was at the instigation of Henry VIII that Tyndale was seized in 1536 and burnt by the Emperor.

impartially hanged people for denying the Royal Supremacy, and burned them for denying Transubstantiation. The gallows were fat in those days : in **1547** the thirty-eight years of Henry's reign about 70,000 persons had been executed, either as criminals or as martyrs.

CHAPTER 12

EDWARD VI AND MARY

THEN came the boy-king, whose reign was to be so 1547-53 short and so momentous. Edward VI was only nine years old when he began to reign; and he died before he

BISHOP LATIMER PREACHING BEFORE EDWARD VI.
(From a contemporary woodcut.)

was fifteen. The country was at first ruled by the Protector Somerset. Archbishop Cranmer was too weak to have commanding influence, but Latimer swayed men's minds by his glorious preaching and by the strength of a fearless heart that was never spoilt by his dazzling

1549 success. Somerset fell in the second year, when the King was only eleven years old, and his power passed to the "subtle ruffian," Northumberland, who had him executed.

The First English Prayer Book

It was now that the authorities began seriously to alter the actual worship and the theology of the Church.

1548 First came the "Order of the Communion" inserted in

1549 the Latin service; then, next year, the *First English Prayer Book.* We need hardly emphasize the importance of this : the services of the Church were now given to the people in a language that they could understand ; and all these services were revised and made into one book, so that everybody could follow what was said, and join in the saying of it.[1]

The Great Pillage

For the rest, the reign of Edward VI was mainly a time of anarchy and horrible plunder—"the plunder of the poor by the rich." [2] Not only in these six years did the ring of robbers who surrounded the throne loot " the immense treasure in the churches, the joy and boast of

---

[1] The reasons for the translation and revision of Divine Service are admirably stated in that second preface of our Prayer Books, which is headed, *Concerning the Service of the Church.*

[2] Dr. Jessopp. It is said that Somerset himself was, like Cranmer, distinguished in that age by his tolerance ; but he certainly was a brigand. He swallowed several churches, and actually seized on Westminster Abbey, designing to use it as building materials for a palace, but the Dean and Chapter bribed him off with twenty manors.

every man and woman and child in England, who day by day and week by week assembled to worship in the old houses of God," [1] but they stripped the friendly societies, benefit clubs, and guilds, of houses and lands and possessions, down to the very tables and chairs; they robbed the almshouses and the hospitals to the last pound,

EDWARD VI AND HIS COUNCILLORS.
(By John Pettie.)

and let the aged go to the roads and the sick to the ditches to wander and to die. The universities only just escaped the general confiscation; the clergy managed to retain some of their endowments, but if the boy-king had lived another three years there is reason to believe that these too would have gone.[2] The peasantry of England has not yet recovered from this awful time, which broke

[1] Dr. Augustus Jessopp, *Before the Great Pillage* (1901), p. 40.
[2] Ibid. pp. 36–40.

its spirit and destroyed its organization. The universities, saved though they were, took years to fill and flourish again. As for the Church, the parish churches of England even to-day are barren and poor compared to what they were before the reign of Edward VI.

Meanwhile the influence of the continental reformers increased rapidly; foreign Protestants who could not speak English were given professors' chairs in the universities. "Calvin, from his pontifical throne at Geneva, directed this motley crew of foreigners, bullied Cranmer, and sought to impose his views on the English Church."[1] John Knox, the Scottish apostle of Calvinism, also came to England in 1551, and was made chaplain to Edward VI.[2] The First Prayer Book was much too

1552 Catholic for these people; therefore, in 1552, the *Second Prayer Book* was published:

"Thus, against the archbishop's will and without the consent of the Church, English religion reached its low-water mark and the ill-starred book of 1552 began its brief career. Ridley officiated at its first use in St. Paul's on All Saints' Day; the choir of St. Paul's was finally devastated, the organ silenced, the bishop in bare rochet, and his clergy in bare surplices filled in the details of the picture; and thereafter all communion ceased except on Sundays."[3]

1553 In the middle of the next year the young King died.

What Queen Mary did

So horrified were the English people at the doings of

[1] Fletcher, *History of England*, vol. ii, p. 103.

[2] It should be remembered in considering the persecutions of the subsequent years that Knox proposed the execution of Gardiner, Bonner, and Tunstall in the interests of Calvinism. Few men were tolerant then.

[3] Procter and Frere, *History of the Book of Common Prayer*, p. 85.

Northumberland and his fellow-miscreants that they welcomed Queen Mary with enthusiasm.

Mary had no thought of persecuting when she began to reign : her early years were happy. But then her own domestic life became unutterably sad : she was neglected by her husband, the cold, hard Philip of Spain ; she realized at last that her dream of having a child to succeed her would never be realized ; and in addition her arms met with defeat abroad. All these things she

BISHOP RIDLEY.   BISHOP LATIMER.

regarded as signs of the Divine wrath, punishing her because she had not been faithful in the extirpation of heresy. So the persecution began : to her morbid, half-Spanish mind it seemed that God's favour might be won by human sacrifices. In this policy she was encouraged by the papal agents ; and the reign that begun so joyfully ended in the profoundest gloom. Altogether, 286 people were martyred at the stake, and they died as Christian heroes ; mostly inoffensive people of humble rank, they

1555

included some saintly parish priests like John Rogers (the first to suffer) and Rowland Taylor, and the five **1555-6** famous martyr-bishops—Cranmer, Latimer, Ridley, Hooper, and Ferrar. Of these the gentle, vacillating Cranmer, for all his faults, is best remembered;

ARCHBISHOP CRANMER ENTERING THE TOWER BY TRAITOR'S GATE.
(By F. Goodall.)

for the gift of his glorious prose in our English Prayer Book is among the greatest of our present possessions.

1553-8 Mary's reign was even shorter than that of Edward. But it accomplished even more. The unhappy woman devoted herself to the cause of Rome, and she succeeded in making the very name of Rome a horror and a detestation. It was she who made the Papacy henceforward for ever impossible in England.

CHAPTER 13

THE ELIZABETHAN SETTLEMENT

THE age of Settlement began with the great Eliza-
bethan era.   In this reign the Church of England
recovered somewhat from the awful ordeals she had gone
through.   The Church maintained her continuity with
the past, and avoided alike the extremes of Mary's
Romanism and also of those foreign Calvinistic reformers
who had dominated the later years of Edward VI.
All the wise statesmanship which marks Elizabeth's long
and prosperous reign was needed to effect a recovery.

1558-
1603

*act of
Supremacy*

A *Third Prayer Book* was soon issued.   In it the
ancient words of administration at the Communion
were restored, and an " Ornaments Rubric " was added
which ordered the use of the old vestments and
ornaments.   A new archbishop was found, in the
wise and moderate Matthew Parker to succeed Cardinal
Pole who had died within a few hours of Queen
Mary.   Great care was taken to safeguard the due
succession, so that the unbroken continuity of the
reformed English Church with the Church of Augustine and Dunstan and Lanfranc should be manifest.
Parker was consecrated by Bishop Barlow (who himself
had been consecrated in the reign of Henry VIII) and
Barlow was assisted by Bishops Coverdale, Scory, and
Hodgkin.   Archbishop Parker did much for the peace of

1559

(1536)

The Consecration of Archbishop Parker in Lambeth Palace Chapel.—By William Dyce.

the Church : he was a learned man who "had studied the Fathers and the Early Church, and he knew that neither Rome nor Geneva could bear to be judged by that test, and that England could."[1]

The Papal Schism

There was need for peace : the Church was harassed by attacks both from Rome without and from the Puritans within. Pope Pius V issued a bull excommunicating the **1570** Queen, and calling upon his followers to rebel against her, and to sever themselves completely from the English Church. This made the breach with Rome, and caused many of those who still acknowledged the authority of the Pope to be cruelly executed as traitors because they, as agents of the Roman mission, went about England inciting the rebellion against the Queen. The attacks of **1588** Rome were, however, much weakened for the time by the defeat of the Armada.

The Puritans

The Church was also harassed from within by the growing power of the Puritans, who, it must be remembered, worked then inside the Church, and were not Dissenters claiming toleration, but Churchmen endeavouring (like everybody else at the time) to oust every opinion but their own. Their influence in high places is seen in the pulling down of the altars in defiance of the law, and many other violent acts. Many people also had a prejudice against the officiating minister wearing beautiful clothes—one of the oddest freaks of the English mind in a period when people had lost

[1] J. H. Overton, *The Church in England* (1897), vol. i, p. 436.

The Spanish Armada.—From a contemporary print.

their balance of mind and humanity. Thus the Puritan clergy objected violently even to wearing the surplice, the cope, and black gown. In the first part of the reign all religion was at a low ebb; but it gradually revived. The Church gained greatly in strength; and, as the reign went on, there arose eminent defenders

RICHARD HOOKER.

of her historic Faith — J e w e l, whom Bishop Creighton calls "one of the great writers of Anglicanism";

† 1571

Hooker, a foremost name in English literature and the principal formulator of the Anglican position; and Andrewes, scholar and saint. But the Puritan storm was brewing all the while.

BISHOP ANDREWES.
(From the Portrait in the Bodleian Library.)

† 1600

† 1626

James I : The Bible

Meanwhile in James I's reign the Church's position was much strengthened by a brilliant succession of good and learned men, who helped to further the settlement. There was perhaps no age in which scholarship was so abundant in the Church, and none in which English was better written. The Prayer Book was revised in James's reign, and thus we had our *Fourth Prayer Book*; but the

1603–25

1604

The Translators presenting the Bible to James I.—By G. E. Kruger-Gray.

chief product of the reign was the *Authorized Version of the Bible*, which was due to the zeal of the King himself.

The Bibles in use had been the " Great Bible "[1] of 1539, which had been followed in 1557–60 by the " Geneva Bible," and in 1568 by the not very successful " Bishops' Bible." After the Hampton Court Conference, at which the Puritans took part, in 1604, it was decided to revise the translation of the Bible again. The Great Bible of 1539 was the real basis of this work.[2] There were forty-seven revisers engaged in what Fuller calls the " hard, heavy, and holy task ": they included the best scholars of the day ; among them Abbot, a Puritan Churchman, now just made Archbishop of Canterbury, Bishop Andrewes and Dr. Overall, who wrote also the last part of the Catechism with its famous definition of the Sacraments. Thus was finished the noble Authorized 1611 Version of the Bible, the greatest literary monument of the English language.

[1] The Great Bible was founded upon Tyndale's Bible, which in its turn had been founded upon the paraphrases of Erasmus.

[2] The style of the Great Bible can easily be compared with that of the Authorized Version, because the Prayer Book Version of the Psalms is that of the Great Bible.

CHAPTER 14

THE CHURCH AND THE PURITANS

THE great controversy between the Church and Puritanism is the outstanding event of the 17th century. At last the indomitable strength of the

The 2 of May. 1643. y Croſſe in Cheapeſide was pulled downe, a Troope of Horſe & 2 Companies of foote wayted to garde it & at y fall of y tope Croſſe dromes beat trupets blew & multitudes of Capes warre throwne in y Ayre. & a greate Shoute of People with ioy, y 2 of May the Almanake ſareth, was y invention of the Croſſe. & 6 day at night was the Leaden Popes burnt, in the pla-ce where it ſtood with -ringinge of Bells, & a greate Acclamation & no hurt done in all theſe actions.

PURITANS PULLING DOWN CHEAPSIDE CROSS UNDER
MILITARY PROTECTION, 1643.
(From a pamphlet of 1648.)

Puritans brought them to power ; and the removal of all fear of foreign invasion gave them freedom to act. They used their power, not to secure toleration (no one outside a tiny cultured circle believed in toleration then), but to

establish Calvinistic Presbyterianism and to make even
the private use of the Prayer Book a penal offence.

Charles I was one of the most moral and religious
men who ever ruled in England; but his autocratic ideas
and unwise statesmanship
made him the last person
to deal with Puritanism,
and rendered the Parlia-
mentarian opposition ne-
cessary and the Civil War
inevitable. In 1643 epis-
copacy was abolished; **1643**
the House of Commons
abolished the Book of **1645**
Common Prayer two years
later. Then Calvinism **1646**
was set up in place of
the moderate and tolerant
Thirty-nine Articles of the
Church. Calvinism may
be briefly described as
the Gospel of Damna-
tion: it taught that the
vast majority of mankind
are predestined to unend-
ing torment and perdition,
not for their own fault,

Officer of Pikemen A.D.
1   6   4   5.

but by the will of God: it thus depraved the very
nature of God Himself. There is not an intelligent
Nonconformist at the present day who does not repudiate
Calvinism as heartily as we Churchmen. Yet this was
the religion which was set up by the Puritans instead
of the Catholic Faith.

1655   A little later on, the Protector, Oliver Cromwell, made it a penal offence to use the Prayer Book even in a private house. Any priest doing this, or acting as a private tutor, was to be banished.   Christmas

10. of May the Boocke of Sportes vpon the Lords day was burnt by the Hangman in the place where the Crosse stoode, & at Exhange

THE BOOK OF SPORTS BURNT BY THE COMMON HANGMAN, 1643.

(This Book, issued by James I, reissued and strongly defended by King Charles, encouraged dancing and games on Sunday—a practice which the Puritans greatly resented.)

(From a contemporary print.)

Day also was prohibited (which led to riots) ; and a law was made forbidding all religious services at marriages. Cromwell is often called an apostle of toleration ; and he *was* tolerant, compared with most other men of his time—but the age was too strong even for him.   The clergy were driven out of their parishes to wander in extreme poverty. Nearly all the bishops suffered imprisonment : Wren, Bishop of Ely, a noted High Churchman, the uncle of Christopher Wren, the architect, was imprisoned in the Tower for twenty years.

Archbishop Laud himself had already been beheaded on Tower Hill.   Laud saved the English Church, as we know it, from being destroyed.   He refused, says

ARCHBISHOP LAUD.
By Vandyck, at Lambeth Palace.

Dr. S. R. Gardiner, to submit his mind to the dogmatism of Puritanism and appealed to the cultivated intelligence for the solution of religious problems. He also secured decent and orderly worship as a principle. Certain marks stand out before the mental vision of the educated churchgoer—the scars indeed of the Great Pillage and of the Puritan Iconoclasm (which wrecked the beauty of our churches more than aught in the 16th century), but also the gifts of Cranmer and of Laud, two Primates of All England, who both died for the Church.

MUSKETEER OF THE ROYAL ARTILLERY COMPANY UNDER THE COMMONWEALTH.

1649   Four years after Laud's death, Charles also was beheaded : he earned the title of King Charles the Martyr because he could at any time have saved his life if he would have deserted the Church.

Then followed the eleven years of the Commonwealth, during which England was ruled by the power of Oliver Cromwell's sword. It must be remembered that though the men who made the "Commonwealth" had rightly struck at the royal absolutism, they were not themselves either democratic or constitutional. During the Commonwealth there was no free General Election, because it was known that the nation would have returned a Royalist majority to Parliament. England welcomed the Restoration of Charles II with enthusiasm in 1660, not only because it was the

THE EXECUTION OF CHARLES I.—(From a contemporary print.)

1660 restoration of Church and King, but more still because it was the restoration of free parliamentary government.

The Restoration, 1660

England was indeed sick of Presbyterian Calvinism, and rejoiced at the Restoration of the Church. A con-

1661 ference was held with the Puritan divines, at the Savoy; but it showed no possibility of agreement. Next year

1662 the Prayer Book was revised, and several improvements made. This was the *Fifth English Prayer Book*, and it is the book we still use to-day, for there has been no revision since. Thus the Reformation era

(1534 1662) was completed. But alas! in the reaction the Puritans were treated with harsh intolerance, and they, as "nonconformists," were forced to become "dissenters," separate from the English Church.

JOHN COSIN (1594–1671), BISHOP OF DURHAM, 1660, IN HIS DOCTOR'S COPE.

(One of the Revisers of the Prayer Book in 1661. From a portrait at Auckland Castle.)

Work of the 17th Century

The 17th century was an age of great scholars, one of whom, Bishop Cosin, had much to do with the preservation and improvement of the Prayer Book. All the fierce opposition which the Church endured had made men study the Anglican position, and compare it carefully with the teaching of the Bible and the Fathers. Thus the opposition and persecution really strengthened the Church in the end. Among the names of these great Anglican divines are those of Jeremy Taylor, Hammond, Bramhall, Barrow, Fuller, Pearson, Stillingfleet. With them let us mention the immortal Puritan writers Baxter and Bunyan ; for the *Saints' Rest* and *Pilgrim's Progress* live to-day with Taylor's *Holy Living* and *Holy Dying*, and the poems of the saintly George Herbert. May they dwell in holy fellowship in a heaven where controversies are forgotten ! It was an age of splendid literature. Shakespeare wrote all his greatest plays in the 17th century ; Milton was a Puritan leader, though he did not hold the orthodox Puritan theology. With Bacon and his *Essays* may be mentioned three devoted Churchmen whose works hold the very front rank of English prose :—Isaac Walton ; Fuller, who wrote the *Worthies* ; and Sir Thomas Browne, the physician, whose *Religio Medici* shows how the best minds kept the breadth and balance of the Catholic Faith even in an age of narrow extremes and furious controversy.

JEREMY TAYLOR.

(From an old engraving.)

GEORGE HERBERT AT BEMERTON.

The Seven Bishops

With a Romanist King, in the person of James II, the **1685–9**
scene changes : for now the last stage was reached in the
long struggle with Rome. The real weakness of the
Anglican position—and the strength of the Puritan—had
been the dependence of the Church upon the Crown, and
the doctrine of the Divine Right of Kings, relics of Tudor

THE SEVEN BISHOPS GOING TO THE TOWER.
(From a contemporary woodout.)

despotism. But when James II tried to thrust **Popery** **1688**
upon England, even the bishops turned against the King.
Seven of them—Sancroft Archbishop of Canterbury, the
saintly Ken (whose morning and evening hymns are sung
wherever the English tongue is spoken), with White,
Lloyd, Turner, Lake, and Trelawney—were charged, and
imprisoned in the Tower. The clergy and people of

England, Nonconformists and Churchmen alike, were solid behind them ; and when at length they were acquitted, they were received with a frenzy of enthusiasm such as has never, alas ! been awakened since.

For an age of quiet decline lay before Christendom.

THE SEVEN BISHOPS RETURNING FROM THE TOWER AFTER
THEIR ACQUITTAL.
(From a contemporary woodcut.)

CHAPTER 15

THE EIGHTEENTH CENTURY

O F the revival in the eighteenth century we shall speak anon. The lowest point was reached in the "dreary days of the first two Georges," and, in spite of **1714-60** the revival which followed, the Church sank to an even lower point in the reign of the last, George IV.   **1820-7**

Causes of the Decline

We have given the names of the Seven Bishops. Of these, in the next year, four, including Archbishop San- **1689** croft and Thomas Ken, refused to take the oath of allegiance to William III when James was deposed. In *Mary* company with four hundred priests and many of the best laymen they were cut off from the Church, and became the *Non-jurors*. They were High Churchmen, who had just saved England from the Pope ; and the loss to the Church of this scholarly and saintly element was incalculable. Henceforth the Church was ruled by Whigs and Latitudinarians until recent times. During the reigns of George I and George II Tory Churchmen were suspected of sympathy with Jacobit- ism, the cause of the Pretenders, and so were out in the cold. Thus did the Church pay heavily for having identified herself with one side in politics during the 17th century. The hand of the now triumphant Whigs lay heavy upon her : worldly men of more than doubtful orthodoxy were made bishops. In George I's reign *Convocation* (the Church's parlia- **1717** ment) was suppressed ; and thus, until it was revived in 1852, the Church had no means of expressing herself : the " Establishment " was represented by those uncon-

CONVOCATION: THE UPPER HOUSE IN 1623.
(From a contemporary print.)

The scene is King Henry VII's Chapel in Westminster Abbey. The Archbishop of Canterbury is in the Chair : he and the other bishops of the Province wear hoods with very large capes over their rochets. In the left-hand corner are four prelates wearing their ordinary outdoor dress of rochet, chimere, and tippet : these are the Archbishop of York and three other visitors from the Northern Province. All wear the square cap.

genial bishops in enormous sleeves whose portraits abound in our picture-galleries ; and it was dominated for many years by the small and selfish Whig aristocracy that really ruled England.

The spirit of the age was also destructive of religious zeal and devotion. Scepticism was the fashion. The author of *Gulliver's Travels* tells us in a famous pamphlet that the system of the Gospel was looked upon as

1708

"generally antiquated and exploded."[1]   The great
Bishop Butler, somewhat later, says that many people   **1736**
take it for granted that Christianity "is now at length
discovered to be fictitious."[2]   The schisms and controversies of the 17th century had sickened many
of religion altogether.   They had also produced in the

CONVOCATION : THE LOWER HOUSE IN 1623.
(From a contemporary print.)

The scene is another part of Westminster Abbey.   The clergy wear their outdoor dress,
gown, tippet, and square cap, over the cassock.   The Dean of Winchester as Prolocutor is in
the Chair.

general public a strong reaction against both Puritanism
and Popery, which showed itself in a horror of "enthusiasm," a worship of moderation in its flabbiest form,
and a singular narrowness of outlook : "the mind of
the 18th century was stiff and unbending to the last
degree ; or rather there was in it a disastrous mixture of
laxity in practice and narrowness in theory."   It was an

[1] Jonathan Swift, *The Abolishing of Christianity*.
[2] Joseph Butler, Advertisement to the *Analogy*.

age of "decent mediocrity." [1]   The Church was alive ; but it was living on its capital.

Men made no attempt to carry out the Prayer Book system.   That expresses the position in a sentence. The English Church had indeed a strong life of a kind, but it had lost hold of the spirit of the Church Catholic. It was not Low Church in the good sense of being evangelical, but in the bad sense of being no-church.

The poor were neglected, and had relapsed largely into barbarism [2] : there was an appalling amount of worldliness among the clergy.   Daily services, after the bright period of Queen Anne's reign, were given up ; the Holy Communion was generally celebrated about three times a year ; very few new churches

The Sleeping Congregation.
(By Hogarth, 1736.)

[1] Overton and Relton, *History of the English Church*, vol. vii, p. 212.
[2] Evidence of this is abundant.   Here let us content ourselves with an extract from Wesley's Journal (Feb. 8, 1753, London) : "I visited many of the sick ; but such scenes, who could see unmoved ?   There are none such to be found in a pagan country.   If any of the Indians in Georgia were sick (which indeed rarely happened till they learned gluttony and drunkenness from the Christians,) those that were near him gave him whatever he wanted.   O who will convert the English into honest Heathen ! "

were built, and the old churches were allowed to be dreary, damp, and rotten.[1] What the ecclesiastical standard was like may be inferred from the fact that Bishop Butler was seriously accused of being a Romanist, because he had a white marble cross on a slab over the altar in his private chapel.

The Methodist Revival

Into this cool atmosphere there burst the fire of two **c. 1745** great revivals. No one would have thought religion dead who, about the year 1745, had seen John Wesley riding forty, or fifty, or even sixty miles a day, reading as he rode, and sometimes preaching five times in one day to vast audiences that were groaning and shouting with excitement. No one would have thought that the age lacked unction and enthusiasm who had seen George Whitefield preaching till even the cynical Lord Chester-field wept, or had seen him holding spellbound in the open fields some 10,000 people, "many of them colliers with whom few dared to mingle." That phrase about the colliers throws a lurid light on the condition of the masses.

It is curious how nearly Wesley's life corresponds with the century which he came to dominate. He was born in 1703, and he lived on in his amazing activity, rising **1703** at four in the morning, and travelling and preaching as usual, until the week of his death in 1791. The service of God that was carried on so long had begun very early: he had been a communicant since he was a child of eight. While George I still lived, Wesley, then a young priest **1726** and Oxford don, had gathered together a few young men

[1] See e.g. Bishop Secker's Fourth Charge (1750), ibid. pp. 289-90.

who were called Methodists because of their strict observance of rules. Thus does revival begin in the midst of decay, and the spring buds appear when the autumn leaves are falling. In 1735 he went as a **1735** missionary to Georgia, tramping through forests, wading and swimming through marshes and rivers, sleeping often on the ground, to awake with frozen **1738-** hair and clothes. In 1738 he **91** was back in England, and there worked till his death, with the motto, "The world is my parish." Naturally enough, his ubiquity produced some resentment; but on the whole the bishops were kind to him.

JOHN WESLEY.
(From the portrait at Christ Church, Oxford.)

Still it took many years, even of Wesley and the Methodists, to make any im- **1760** pression upon that age. When George III came to the throne there was no general improvement perceptible, nor was there much to be discerned during the next ten years or so. But by the end of the century it may be claimed that Wesley's influence had revived religion; had begun the restoration of the common people out of the half-savage condition into which they had sunk since the Great Pillage and the Reformation; and had changed the moral tone of all society, so that, for instance, bribes were no longer taken by respectable politicians—which is significant of much. But even Wesley did not cure that innate defect of the age, the absence of Church principles. He was himself a strong Churchman, and he broke with White-field because of the latter's Calvinism :

"He was a Church of England man even in circumstantials. There was not a service or a ceremony, a gesture or a habit, for which he had not an unfeigned predilection." [1]

He designed Methodism to be a religious guild within the Church. Other revivals, he said, on laying the foundation-stone of the City Road Chapel, had soon "formed themselves into a distinct sect," and thus "the generality of the English nation were little profited thereby "; but the Methodists were " to continue in the Church, maugre men or devils." And two years before his death he made an impassioned appeal :

"In God's name, stop ! Ye yourselves were just called to the Church of England, and although you have a thousand temptations to leave it and set up for yourselves, regard them not. Be Church of England men still. Do not cast away the peculiar glory which God hath put upon you, and frustrate the design of Providence, the very end for which God hath raised you up."

But, alas ! the " spirit of the age " was too strong for him. The Methodists did " form themselves into a distinct sect "; and are now one of the largest of the Nonconformist bodies, separate from us until God's Providence shall unite us again.

The Evangelical Revival

The Evangelical Revival, which followed on the Methodist, remained a revival within the Church, though it adopted the Calvinism of Whitefield in a modified form, and had not Wesley's grasp of Church principles. During the last quarter of the 18th century the

[1] Alexander Knox, " who knew him perhaps better than any man did " (quoted by Overton and Relton, p. 91).

Evangelicals were the salt of the English Church ; and when we speak of Wesley's great influence we must remember that much of this influence was now represented by them. They fought their way through contempt and opposition, and it was mainly they who by the end of the century had changed the tone of the Church and of England as a whole. Evangelicalism filled the Church with saints ; men like † 1807 John Newton, the converted slave-trader ; women like Hannah More, whose books and tracts had an enormous influence, and whose personal work in c. 1790 Somerset fought down the barbarous paganism of the people [1] ; and many other splendid Christians—Fletcher † 1785 of Madeley, the Swiss soldier who became a Methodist and the most saintly of English parish priests; Henry Venn ; and Romaine ; and the poet Cowper—to mention only those whose names are best known.

But principally are the Evangelicals remembered for the spirit of philanthropy which they created and brought to such enduring results. The redemption by education of the long-neglected masses was begun by Robert 1781 Raikes, the founder of Sunday Schools (which came into existence for the teaching of the three 'R's). So too, at the 1799 end of the century Rowland Hill [2] founded the Religious Tract Society. But greater than these efforts at civilizing

[1] It Cheddar, for instance, there was only one Bible, and that was used to prop up a flowerpot : there had not been a resident minister for over forty years ; "and every house was a scene of ignorance and vice."

[2] Six bishops had refused to ordain him, between 1769 and 1773, because of his "irregular" proceedings as an undergraduate in preaching at the villages about Cambridge. He then was ordained deacon, but, as he would not give up open-air preaching, he was refused priest's orders. He lived till 1833.

England was the Emancipation of the Slaves by William Wilberforce and his friends of the Clapham sect, including Clarkson the Quaker, Henry Thornton the rich banker (who gave away six-sevenths of his large income till he **1759-1833** was married, and then gave two-thirds), and John Venn, son of Henry Venn, and Rector of Clapham. Wilberforce began the fight as Member of Parliament in 1787 : after twenty years of **1807** struggle these men converted the nation, and the Act for the Abolition of the Slave Trade was passed. Three days before his death Wil- **1833** berforce heard that England was ready to pay twenty millions for the emancipation of the slaves, and the Act for this also was passed.

WILLIAM WILBERFORCE.

Toleration

Two causes, perhaps the two greatest in Christendom, also grew up in the despised 18th century—Missionary Work and Toleration. Of the latter we need say little. We owe Toleration mainly to the Latitudinarian spirit ; for it must be remembered that there is a noble and true Latitudinarianism, which is not indifference and low belief, but the desire to include as many as possible in the Christian fellowship, and to avoid driving those who differ from us out of the Church. Every one knows that now all men are free and have equal rights, while once they could be cruelly persecuted for their religious opinions. Between 1718 and 1813 the still severe penal laws against Protestant and especially against Roman Catholic Nonconformists were removed; and in 1858 Jews were allowed parliamentary rights.

Missionary Work

It is strange that England should have sent out no missionaries between Anglo-Saxon times and the Jacobean Era. The British Church, after producing men like Patrick, David, and Ninian, had ended in quiescence. The English Church did little after the age of St. Boniface, and from the 10th century to the 16th the voice of the missionary was only heard in the Eastern Church : during the Middle Ages, when the Churches in communion with Rome seemed so strong and secure, they were making no progress, but were shrinking before the advancing hordes of Mohammedanism.[1] In the sixteenth century St. Francis Xavier and other Roman Catholics carried out very wonderful missionary work. But we in England did almost nothing during the horrible controversies of the 16th and 17th centuries. Then, just at the close of the latter century, Dr. Thomas Bray, with some friends, founded the Society for Promoting Christian Knowledge, which was from the first a missionary society as well as a society to revive that work of teaching the people which had fallen so low since the Reformation. Shortly afterwards the indefatigable Dr. Bray, with the help of Archbishop

1698

S.P.C.K.

---

[1] Mohammed was founding his religion at the very time when St. Augustine landed in England in 597. In 1453 the Turks conquered the chief city of Eastern Christendom, Constantinople, and have held it ever since. Spain was a Mohammedan country from 711 till 1492—a strange fact to remember.

Tenison and others, founded the Society for the Propaga-   1701
tion of the Gospel, which was the first great systematic   S. P. G.
missionary effort in the English Church since Anglo-
Saxon times.   During the 18th
century missionary endeavour
grew, though slowly : vast
opportunities were missed ;
America, for instance, had not
a single bishop to ordain and
confirm till after the War of
Independence, when Bishop
Seabury was consecrated, and   1784
even this had to be done by

BISHOP BUTLER.

BISHOP BERKELEY.

Scottish prelates.   None the
less, the new work did grow,
and missions were founded
in most non-Christian countries during the 18th century.
Last of all, as a result of the
Evangelical fervour at the
close, the Church Missionary   1799
Society was launched upon
its grand career.

There were also famous
Churchmen, not specially connected with the movements
we have mentioned —— laymen like Dr. Johnson and
Burke, prelates like the saintly Bishop Wilson, the great

Bishop Butler, the still greater Bishop Berkeley ; priests like William Law, the author of the *Serious Call*, who belonged to no party, but was a Catholic mystic, from whom John and Charles Wesley and their fellows learnt much—and of whom Dr. Johnson himself was a disciple. To Law may also be traced the movements of the 19th century, from that of the Tractarians to those which are about us even now. His spirit lives on, and his books will last for ever.

CHAPTER 16

THE NINETEENTH CENTURY

THE English Church since the Reformation has been like an old garden gradually recovering from the havoc of a steamplough. This does not mean that the Reformation was not necessary or at least inevitable : how necessary we think it was will depend upon how much we think the ground had got trodden and hard and weedy ; and people naturally have different opinions about this. But most certainly the havoc was great, and attended with a vast amount of unnecessary hatred, violence, narrowness, and destruction. Now, in a garden roughly treated, many plants once a very part of the soil disappear, and are slowly and with difficulty established again : in some parts the flowers may grow better than ever ; but there are many waste places, because it takes years for multitudes of precious plants to recover their native growth. Thus summers and winters pass, times of growth, times of hidden incubation—ups-and-downs, as it seems, during which the garden matures again. So it has been with the Church. More especially during that century of controversy which we call the Reformation the common people lost the common faith, lost the religious tradition, drifted away from their ancient intimacy with the things of God. The common people have indeed been like shy plants which are difficult to re-establish.

Now, this aloofness of the people was the great weakness of the English Church. Methodism, as we have seen, bravely tackled it ; but, just because the tradition of Church principles had been lost, both Methodism and Evangelicalism failed to rebuild the walls of Jerusalem. They converted many men of all classes ; they brought a new spirit into England : but they did not make a Church of the English people.

A Cheerless Dawn

And so, in spite of all that had been done by those devoted men, the 19th century opened blackly for the Church—blackly for religion altogether. The Church herself proved to be far weaker than ever before. At the beginning of the 18th century there were twenty-four Churchmen to every Dissenter ; but at the beginning of the 19th century there were only four Churchmen to every Dissenter. We rejoice to-day at the good work which our Nonconformist brethren did when the Church was slack, and are still doing. We love them for their devotion to our common Master ; but our love would be a poor thing if it did not make us sad that they are separated from us, and if it did not make us long for the time when all barriers between us and them will be broken down.

The net result, then, of the Methodist and Evangelical revivals had been a great disintegration of the old national religion : the Evangelicals had attached little importance to their churchmanship, and the nation had taken them at their word. They had pressed the individualist side of religion, and had passed over that corporate aspect of which the Gospels are so full.   Moreover, their restricted outlook upon life caused a reaction against religion in the creative worlds of literature and art ; and they had no influence on thought—they were not intellectual or learned men, they produced not a single book of permanent value. Now the science and thought and literature of the 19th century were going to prove a mighty power that would shrivel up any religion which was not wise and profound. Clearly, further movements would be needed if the Church was to cope with the thought of the modern world, and to answer its needs.

The 19th century opened blackly; for the Church had no hold upon the people. There had been a great shaking of dry bones, but the body was not yet formed again : the 18th century had done nothing to restore the Prayer Book system, to recover England to Church ways ; of parish work as we understand it there was little or none, except for saintly men here and there who did good in their own way ; there was still no general method, and the average parish priest was respectably inefficient, while the churches were dismally undevotional. The work of rebuilding Jerusalem was indeed really going forward : the National Society began to educate the English people in 1811 ; the first bishop was sent to India in 1814. Yet there was no open vision in those days : the clergy did not understand Church principles or know how to proceed. The Church excited no enthusiasm.

Indeed the Church was so unpopular between 1820 and 1833 that bishops spoke openly in their charges about her approaching destruction. "Four years," said the Bishop of Lichfield, "must elapse now before we meet again on a similar occasion, and I feel that a more

1800–
33

L

than common uncertainty hangs over such a prospect" :
"Set your house in order!" said Lord Grey to the
bishops in the House of Lords ; and in the Commons
Joseph Hume spoke of the Church as "a body condemned by the country," whose "charter was on the
eve of being cancelled by the authority that gave it"—
a delightful example of the current Erastianism ; "he
also hoped that young
gentlemen would not in-
vest in such a condemned
building" as the Church
of England by becoming
clergymen, and that "these
foolish ordinations would
terminate." Bishops were
burnt in effigy : the Bishop
of London was warned that
it was dangerous for him
to preach in a London
church ; the Bishop of
Bristol's palace was razed
to the ground by an
infuriated mob. "The
Church of England," said

"Bishops were burnt in effigy."

Mr. T. Mozley,"was folding its robes to die with what
dignity it could." [1]

The Catholic Revival

1833   Then in 1833 John Keble (six years after he had
published the *Christian Year*), preached his Assize

[1] The subject is well discussed in Canon Overton's *Church in
England*, vol. ii, chap. xi.

Sermon on " National Apostasy," and the Oxford Movement was begun. It did not indeed at first increase the
popularity of the Church : on the contrary, the " Tracts   1833-
for the Times," which caused the name of Tractarians to   40
be given to Newman, Pusey, Keble, and their comrades,
though they roused eager enthusiasm in many, caused

also the wildest fury of opposition, which resulted, soon
after the last of the tracts, in   1845
Newman seceding to the
Church of Rome. Many
other good men went with
him ; and we in our time,
when a generation has passed
since any Church leader or
theologian of eminence has
followed his example, can
hardly imagine the alarm
which was caused by the
secessions of 1845 and the
following years.

The opposition was great ;
for the Tractarians not only
went against the manners of
their age, as the Methodists
and Evangelicals had done
—they also went clean against

DR. PUSEY.

its most deep-seated religious prejudices. They harked
back behind the 18th century to the great divines
of the English Church—Andrewes, Laud, Bramhall,
Jeremy Taylor, Cosin, and the rest ; and they
demanded that England should be Catholic : they
showed too what was the teaching of those " ancient

Fathers" of the Church Universal to whom the Prayer Book appeals ; and they showed how the greatest intellects of the 18th century itself—men like Water-land, Butler, and Law—were with them. They demanded, to use their own words, the full "doctrine and discipline" of the English Church ; they reminded their fellow country-men that they professed in the Creed to believe in the Catholic Church. And this, in an age when that doctrine and disci-pline had been for generations in abeyance, and the plainest directions of the Prayer Book ignored, and when men used the word "Catholic" as synony-mous with Romanism — this sounded like flat Popery. John

JOHN KEBLE.
(1792–1866.)

Bull was seriously alarmed. It wanted a good deal of courage to be a "Puseyite."

Amid all the opposition, the cause proceeded with astonishing depth and strength. The tracts penetrated into every parsonage ; the personal influence of the learned and saintly Tractarians raised up at once a generation of young men devoted to their cause, laymen like Gladstone, priests like Dean Church. It was the greatest revolution since the Reformation. Men believed again in the Church—in the Church not as a national establishment, flanked by the lion and unicorn, but as a holy fellowship, the Kingdom of Heaven upon earth, as set forth by Christ in the Gospels. The religion of the Prayer Book was restored again. At a time when the Fall and the Atonement had been for long preached almost to the exclusion of other things, at a time when the ordinary religious teaching of pious ordinary people had been for generations an almost quaint form of Judaism,[1] the Gospel of the Incarnation was preached through the length and breadth of the land, and men began again really to believe in the Sacraments.

All this has now become part of the very texture of our Churchmanship. The names " High," " Low," " Broad," " Moderate," still survive amongst us ; but the members of all these parties now for the most part agree in holding views about the Church and the Sacraments which fifty years ago would have been considered Puseyite. So it has been with external things. A religion without external manifestations may be the religion of a clique of scholars, but it cannot be the religion of a people. The Catholic Revival grew almost suddenly, **1859** after its reverses at Oxford, into a so-called "Ritualistic" movement ; in Cambridge especially, whence came the immortal hymn-writer, Dr. Neale, and other leaders, the study of art and of liturgical knowledge grew up, so that the Cambridge Movement really popularized the Oxford Movement. Church principles began to be understood and practised among the people in many parish churches. There was again violent opposition, much injustice and persecution—priests were even imprisoned ; but victory

---

[1] Let the reader pick up any old-fashioned book that belonged to his grandparents and look at the curious woodcuts and letterpress, if he wishes to realize how very Judaistic was the undenominationalism of those days.

came to the men who gave up all prospects of advance-
ment, and served the poor.   At the present day a ceremonial and symbolism, which caused riots forty years
ago, is used by Low as well as High Churchmen, and
much of it has even been introduced by Presbyterians
and Methodists in their worship.   No one now denies
that beauty is one of God's attributes.

YORK MINSTER.

But, further than this, it is becoming abundantly
clear, not only among Churchmen, but among thought-
ful Christians generally, that in the future the one
alternative to a vague theism will be Catholicism, a
broad and universal Faith—not a religion that believes
only in the Protestant ideas of three centuries, or that
believes only in the Church of Rome, for each is precisely
the denial of the Holy Church Universal—but a belief
in that large and humane fellowship, which is inspired
by the Holy Ghost, and is the Body whose Head is
Christ.

New Life in the Church

The Church Revival broadened the Church of England : it did not destroy the work of the earlier Caroline, Latitudinarian, and Evangelical movements, but added to them what was lacking. Notably also it brought religion back to the people. It may be truly said of the last fifty years that " the poor have the Gospel preached to them."

Men of all shades of opinion plunged into the great congested centres of population, where the clergy had been almost unknown before and certainly unloved. Parochial activity began again ; and the work of recovering the masses of our people was taken in hand. It is a long task, to be accomplished only by sheer devotion and the patient hope of generations ; for very many are still hardly Christian except in name. Those who believe most in the Reformation have the greatest reason for removing this enormous blot on its work—that, before it, all Englishmen joined in the worship of God, and that, since, the common people (who had not been consulted when the Reformation was carried out) drifted away, at first, as we have said, into something very like barbarism, and then into their present materialism and indifference.

FREDERICK DENISON
MAURICE.
(1805–1872.)

The Church Revival, among all shades of opinion, has also restored that half of the Christian religion which was lost sight of in the days of Calvinistic individualism—the Duty to our Neighbour. The names of Frederick Maurice and Kingsley will always be remembered in connection with this great revival of social duty ; and the name of the Evangelical Lord Shaftesbury shines brightly in the pages of history, because he destroyed the horrible " white slavery " in our factories, and thus carried on the social work which Wilberforce and his friends had begun by the destruction of the black slavery abroad. To-day there are few Churchmen who do not realize to some extent our duty in ameliorating the lot of Christ's poor, and the nation as a whole now understands how valuable is the Church's work in this sacred cause.

CHARLES KINGSLEY.

In every department a wonderful activity now exists. The Revival of Convocation in 1852, the starting of Church Congresses, the many societies and associations for reform and for good works, have produced already admirable results, which were illustrated in a thrilling way by the great Pan-Anglican Congress of 1908, when there assembled 242 bishops from all parts of the world, with a vast body of priests, laymen, and women, representing the Anglican Church in Europe, Asia, Africa, America, and Australasia. The crowded meetings that occupied the principal halls of London for day after day, showed by the wisdom, largeheartedness, and enthusiasm of those present, in the discussion of an astonishingly wide variety of subjects, how profound a change has come over our whole Church during the past century.

Most stirring of all is the response that has been made to the world-problem. We cannot here describe the missionary work of our times. Suffice it to say that whereas in 1800 there were 200 millions of Christians in the world, the number to-day is 500 millions. This astounding increase has been far greater than that of the whole world's population, which has risen by little over 500 millions; and the proportion of Christians to the world-population rose from 20 per cent. in 1800 to 28½

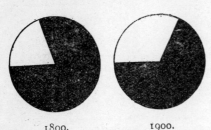

1800.   1900.
THE PROPORTION OF PROFESSING CHRISTIANS TO THE REST OF THE WORLD.
The white spaces represent the Christian populations.
(From an S.P.G. card.)

per cent. in 1875, and to 33⅓ per cent. in 1896. This increase of recent years coincides with the period during which intercessions for Missions has become one of the recognized duties of the Church.

The following figures were given by Bishop Boyd-Carpenter, nearly twenty years ago, in the *Encyclopaedia Britannica* [1] :

A.D.	CHRISTIAN POPULATION.	
100	-	5 millions
200	-	2 ,, (Persecution).
300	-	5 ,,
400	-	10 ,, } (Conversion of England, etc.).
800	-	30 ,,

[1] Vol. 27 (New Vol. 3), p. 54.

A.D.		CHRISTIAN POPULATION.		
1000	-	50 millions.		
1500	-	100	,,	
1600	-	125	,,	
1700	-	155	,,	
1800	-	200	,,	(1,000 millions, population of world).
1875	-	394	,,	(1,396 millions, population of world).
1880	-	410	,,	
1890	-	493	,,	
1896	-	500	,,	(1,500 millions, population of world).
[1] 1907	-	558	,,	

In 1600 about 3½ million square miles were under Christian government. To-day no less than 40 million square miles are under Christian government; that is to say, the Christian nations now rule between 4 and 5 square miles for every 1 square mile ruled by the professors of all other religions put together. That we may understand the responsibility of British and American Churchmen in the matter, let us add this fact to be remembered : in 1800, the English-speaking peoples numbered 20 millions ; in 1890, they numbered 111 millions ; that is to say, the English language is spoken by one out of every fifteen people in the world. How immense are the possibilities before us, if we are true to our Father in heaven !

More profoundly cheering still is the wisdom and charity shown in the mission-field. The world at large has not yet learnt how scientific and thorough, and

---

[1] According to the Blue Book of Missions, 1907.

how broad-minded, practical, and serviceable is the evangelical enthusiasm of our devoted missionary workers. And mission work teaches charity : it is a great preventive of the spirit of schism : it draws Christian men together already in a real unity of spirit.

There were other Church movements in the 19th century which, though less striking, had and still have a profound influence. That century was marked by a huge revolution of thought in the world at large. It was the age of scientific discovery, of historical criticism, of marvellous mechanical invention. The whole world was changed.

It would have been strange if this vast upheaval had not unsettled many minds. The Gospel had not changed ; but the philosophy, the science, the history, through which men had understood the Gospel, were changed enormously. The thought-movement in the Church since Tractarian times has consisted mainly in re-stating the Catholic Faith in the terms of modern knowledge. That work is not yet complete ; nor is this the place to write of it. But it seems to be making for the reunion of Christendom. The narrow bitterness, both Roman and Protestant, of the Reformation period has become impossible to thinking men. The ideal of one holy, Catholic, and reunited Church will become possible to our descendants.

We look back, and we understand at last how goodly is our heritage. We look forward, and we feel how splendid is the future that we Churchmen may share in making.

A LIST OF WORKS ON THE HISTORY OF THE CHURCH OF ENGLAND

---

(1) *English Christianity in its Beginnings.* By Rev. E. H. Pearce. (S.P.C.K. 1s. 9d. net.)

(2) *The Christian Church in these Islands Before the Coming of Augustine,* and *Augustine and his Companions.* Both by the Right Rev. G. F. Browne, D.D. (S.P.C.K. 1s. 9d. net.)

(3) *The Beginnings of English Christianity.* By the Right Rev. W. E. Collins, D.D. (Methuen. 5s. n t.)

(4) *A Short History of the Church in Great Britain.* By the Very Rev. W. H. Hutton, D.D. (Rivingtons. 4s. net.)

(5) *The Church in England.* By the Rev. J. H. Overton, D.D. 2 vols. in the 'National Churches' Series. (Wells Gardner. 3s. 6d. net each.)

(6) *A Popular History of the Church of England from the Earliest Times to the Present Day.* By the Right Rev. W. Boyd Carpenter, D.D. (Murray. 6s. net.)

(7) The series of ' Epochs of Church History.' Edited by the late Bishop Creighton. (Longmans. 3s. 6d. net each.) Especially—

    (a) *Wyclif and the Beginnings of the Reformation.* By R. L. Poole.

(*b*) *The English Church in the Middle Ages.* By the Rev. W. Hunt, D.Litt.

(*c*) *The History of the Reformation in England.* By the Rev. G. G. Perry.

(*d*) *The Church and the Puritans.* By H. O. Wakeman.

(*e*) *The Evangelical Revival.* By the Rev. J. H. Overton, D.D.

(8) Any one who possesses any knowledge of the subject should read *An Introduction to the History of the Church of England,* by H. O. Wakeman (Rivingtons, 7*s.* 6*d.* net), in reality a brilliant essay, delightful in style, reverent in tone, and sane in its judgements.

Those who wish to pursue a more advanced course of study will be able to find books for themselves. But for the detailed study of any period we may recommend the separate volumes of the 'History of the English Church,' edited by the late Dean of Winchester and the Rev. W. Hunt, D.Litt. (Macmillans). 8/6 each.

(*a*) *The English Church from its Foundation to the Norman Conquest.* By the Rev. W. Hunt, D.Litt.

(*b*) „ „ *from the Norman Conquest to the Close of the Thirteenth Century.* By the Very Rev. W. R. W. Stephens, D.D.

(*c*) „ „ *in the Fourteenth and Fifteenth Centuries.* By the Rev. W. W. Capes.

(*d*) „ „ *from the Accession of Henry VIII to the Death of Mary.* By James Gairdner, C.B., LL.D.

(*e*) „ „ *in the Reigns of Elizabeth and James I.* By the Rev. W. H. Frere, D.D.

(*f*) *The English Church from the Accession of Charles I to the Death of Anne.* By the Very Rev. W. H. Hutton, D.D.

(*g*) ,, ,, *from the Accession of George I to the End of the Eighteenth Century.* By the Rev. J. H. Overton, D.D., and the Rev. F. Relton.

(*h*) ,, ,, *in the Nineteenth Century.* By Francis Warre Cornish. 2 Vols. 8*s.* 6*d.* each.

(9) *A Dictionary of English Church History.* Edited by the Rev. S. L. Ollard and Gordon Crosse. (Mowbrays. 15*s.* net.)

Reference may also be made here to Canon Perry's three volumes, entitled the *Student's English Church History* (John Murray. 9*s.* each), which cover the periods 596–1509, 1509–1717, 1717–1884; Dr. Jessopp's *History of the Church of England* (S.P.C.K. 2*d.*)—which, however, only goes down to 1660; and to the many publications of the Church Historical Society (S.P.C.K.). All students should remember, however, that a true understanding of Church History is impossible without a sound basis of general knowledge, such as might be supplied by the late J. R. Green's *Short History of the English People* (Macmillan. 7*s.* 6*d.* net), or the two vivid and entertaining volumes of Mr. Fletcher's *Introductory History of England* (Murray. 7*s.* 6*d.* net each).

PRINTED IN ENGLAND BY
A. R. MOWBRAY AND CO. LTD., LONDON AND OXFORD

A DICTIONARY OF
ENGLISH CHURCH HISTORY

Edited by the
REV. S. L. OLLARD, M.A.

Rector of Bainton, Yorks. ; Hon. Canon of Worcester ;
Examining Chaplain to the Archbishop of York.

Assisted by
GORDON CROSSE, M.A.
Of New College, Oxford, and Lincoln's Inn.

And by nearly Seventy Contributors.

Super Royal 8vo.   690 pp.

With an Appendix and Three Maps.   Second Edition Revised.

Cloth, 15/- net.

"A MAGNUM OPUS.—The warmest congratulations are due to all concerned in the production of this large and admirable book. It is a remarkable illustration of Anglican scholarship, and a book of which the English Church may well be proud."—*Church Times.*

"The work has been well done. . . . It is so brightly written that we feel sure it will be used not only for reference but for continuous reading as well. The editors have been fortunate in securing an excellent list of contributors."—*Times.*

"Its editors are to be congratulated on the result of their labours . . . which contains as much information as one could reasonably expect to find in such a work. The articles are for the most part short, they are never immoderately long; and in spite of the fact that they contain a great deal of matter in a very small space, they are always readable."—*English Historical Review.*

"Learned without being pedantic, popular without being superficial, and combining adequate treatment with the avoidance of excessive length."—*Oxford Magazine.*

A. R. MOWBRAY & CO. LTD., LONDON AND OXFORD